BASICS
INTERACTIVE DESIGN

Dave Wood

INTERFACE DESIGN

AN INTRODUCTION TO VISUAL COMMUNICATION IN
UI DESIGN

T0173258

BLOOMSBURY VISUAL ARTS

LONDON · NEW YORK · OXFORD · NEW DELHI · SYDNEY

BLOOMSBURY VISUAL ARTS
Bloomsbury Publishing Plc
50 Bedford Square, London, WC1B 3DP, UK
1385 Broadway, New York, NY 10018, USA
29 Earlsfort Terrace, Dublin 2, Ireland

BLOOMSBURY, BLOOMSBURY VISUAL ARTS and the Diana logo
are trademarks of Bloomsbury Publishing Plc

First published in Great Britain by Fairchild Books 2014
This edition published by Bloomsbury Visual Arts 2019
Reprinted 2020, 2021, 2023

A catalogue record for this book is available from the British Library.

The Library of Congress has cataloged the Fairchild Books edition as follows:
Wood, David, 1963-
Interface design: an introduction to visual communication in UI design / David Wood
pages cm. — (Basics interactive design)
Includes bibliographical references and index.
ISBN 978-2-940411-99-3 (alk. paper) – ISBN 978-2-940447-57-2
1. User interfaces (Computer systems)—Design—Case studies.
2. Computer programmers—interviews. I. Title.
QA76.9.U83W658 2014
005.4'437—dc23
2013038749

ISBN: PB: 978-1-3501-4085-1
ePDF: 978-2-9404-4757-2
ePUB: 978-1-4742-2945-6

Series: Basics Interactive Design

Printed and bound in Great Britain

To find out more about our authors and books visit
www.bloomsbury.com and sign up for our newsletters.

4 | **Contents**

An interface is the contact point between humans and machines. A user interface (UI) on a computer, smartphone, tablet or game console consists of a 'front-end' visually interactive face that communicates with a programmed delivery system 'back end'. These 'front-end' interfaces are known as graphical user interfaces (GUIs).

A successful UI design blends good usability, functionality and aesthetics to facilitate a successful outcome, based on the user's requirements and expectations. UI designs should therefore focus on a user's needs and expectations, not on what a programmer or designer thinks is logical or cool.

The driver of a car doesn't want to read a hefty manual, or understand the complex mechanical engineering that sits behind the sleek bodywork, or be confused by an overcomplicated dashboard. When they get in the driver's seat they want to turn the ignition key and *drive*. Similarly, anyone confronted with a new UI for the first time wants the outcome of their interaction to be quickly facilitated by good design. This means that the aesthetic and the functional features of the interface must combine to produce a fantastic user experience.

Online resources to accompany this title are available at:

http://tinyurl.com/examplegrid.

Please type the URL into your web browser and follow the instructions to access the Companion Website. If you experience any problems, please contact Bloomsbury at: companionwebsites@bloomsbury.com

Aims

This book aims to do three fresh things for interface design:

Firstly, it will take you through the *hows*, the *whys* and the *wherefores* of designing user interfaces – from a graphic design perspective.

Secondly, it will be an express journey through the importance of user experience and how to design better interactions for humans, not machines.

Thirdly, this book explores design principles and stresses the importance of usability and aesthetics working together – and shows how this can be done. It is not a technical UI book; instead, it provides a visual communication grounding and champions graphic design as a valid standard in interface design.

Most importantly, the book will demonstrate that designing for dynamic user experience means exciting opportunities for creative facilitation of user-control. Designing better interactions for a user does not mean the designer losing control of their aesthetic – far from it.

The terms 'visual designer' and 'visual design' are avoided in this book, although they are often used to describe roles and outputs within interface design. The terms miss the richness of visual communication that a designer from such a background brings to designing interfaces.

The chapters

Chapter 1 focuses on establishing visual communication's key importance in interface design and the designer's responsibility to the user.

Chapter 2 delves into designing for interaction across a range of different graphical user interfaces, before examining information architecture.

Chapter 3 creates a useful framework of important key points on graphic design for digital media – layout, colour, iconography, imagery and typography.

Chapter 4 builds upon this framework and applies these visual communication basics to effectively facilitate a successful interactive user experience.

Chapter 5 provides practical help for designers to improve their communication with the developer by exploring each other's needs.

Finally, in **Chapter 6** the book will conclude by looking at designing for interactivity within our senses and our environment.

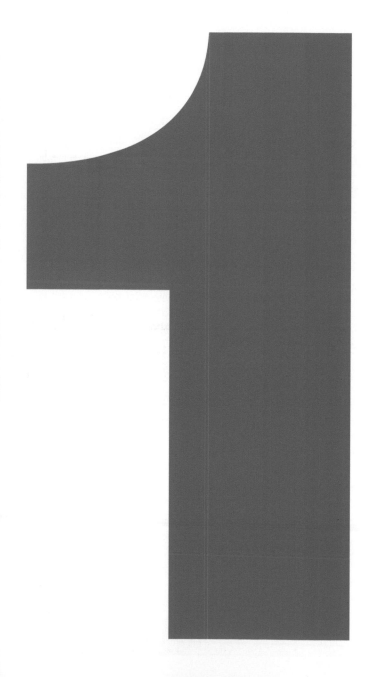

Visual communication: A standard in designing interaction

User interface (UI) design brings together a team of specialists in order to create a successful interactive experience for the user. Jorge Frascara, an internationally renowned professor of communication design, explains visual communication as emphasizing the method *(design)*, the objective *(communication)* and the medium *(visual)* through the manipulation of text and image into a graphical outcome. As such, a graphic designer's visual communication skills are vital in ensuring a UI's aesthetic accessibility. This is done throughout the entire UI design process.

This chapter looks at visual communication as part of the design discipline and also as a standard in designing interaction within a collaborating UI design team.

Interface design is a complex process involving the UI design team, the target users and the client. It is an iterative process, with phases of user research, ideation, testing, building, and further testing, all contributing to the design of an interactive user experience. The graphic designer is important to the design process, but is very much part of a team of other specialists. Graphic designers must be confident in their own specialist knowledge to successfully design the UI's aesthetic, but also have a wider contextual knowledge to communicate with the rest of the team. This communication begins at the ideation stage of the project, well before any code or designs have been developed.

'A good designer sees the organic process where others are chained to the perceived technical limitations or perceived possibilities of a system.'
– Anon

Graphic designers in the UI team

There are often misunderstandings about what a graphic designer can and will contribute to UI design, a common idea being that graphic design simply involves creating graphics to 'skin' the UI code. This 'visual design' decorating phase is expected to come at the end of the project, once the rest of the team has done the 'real work'.

This misconception of what a graphic designer contributes to the UI design, and at what point, stems from an unfortunate focus on the word 'graphic'. Graphic design is not about designing a graphic; it is about designing effective visual communication. This communication is crafted by the graphic designer, through manipulation of text and image, into an aesthetic that is suitable for a particular audience.

Aesthetics is an integral part of the users' experience of any interface. It guides them towards key interactions in the UI, allowing them to achieve their goals. It communicates action and content, making connections between the users' hearts and heads in facilitating their interactive outcomes. Through the graphic designer, visual communication becomes an important standard in UI design, ultimately leading to the design of a better user experience. The aesthetic of the UI engages and holds the attention of the user before any link is clicked or any code is processed. Therefore the graphic designer's skills should be utilized throughout the entire design process, not just at the end.

1.1
Innovative navigation
The synthesis of strong visual communication and engaging coding can create a fantastic user experience. Canadian design company GRIP knows it works. Their website is innovative in its navigation and content delivery, and the strong visual communication attracts and separates the content.
www.griplimited.com

Neither Mars nor Venus

Each specialist in a UI design team has a different contribution to make. Information architects create the interactive structure. User experience (UX) designers create the experience. Developers create clean UI code. Graphic designers communicate the UI's visual hierarchy, functionality and interaction.

In any team, tension between specialists can exist. Within a UI design team, this often comes down to cost implications, different specialist languages and varying perspectives on how to design an interface. If many online forum debates are to be believed, there is particular tension between UI designers and developers. So much that designers could be from Mars and developers from Venus.

It takes effort to see a project from each other's viewpoint, but effective collaboration is a crucial part of designing a successful UI.

A great designer will work within the constraints of the brief – such as budget, accessibility, target user, and available technology – shaping the visual elements of text and image to communicate the content and navigation. Constraints fuel designers to create successful UI design solutions through collaboration with the rest of the UI design team.

The combined work of both designer and developer will be a UI that is coded well and has an aesthetic that attracts, retains attention and is usable. The UI will undergo some form of user testing throughout the design process to ensure this. Usability expert Steve Krug suggests a variety of methods to do this (see his interview on pages 28–31).

The UI design team

A UI design team will ideally include at least:

— An information architect defining the interactive structure

— A user experience designer making the UI usable for both the client and user

— A graphic designer shaping the UI's aesthetic accessibility

— A developer writing the front-end mark-up and the back-end code

1.2
Mars and Venus
Not all design teams succumb to the conflicted view of designers vs developers. Companies such as Athlon Productions believe in close collaboration to achieve successful designs.
www.athlonproduction.com

1.3
User experience
German developer Martin Gauer uses great coding and quality visual communication to create innovative and successful user experiences.
http://attackemart.in

1.2

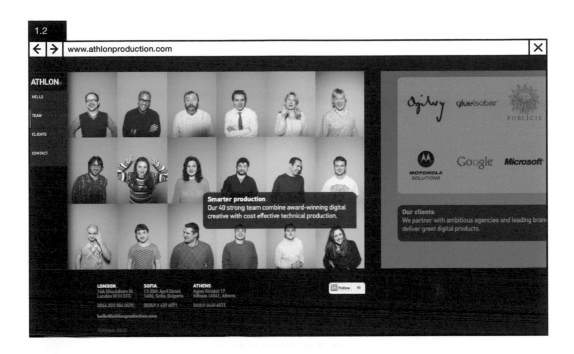

← → www.athlonproduction.com ✕

ATHLON

HELLO

TEAM

CLIENTS

CONTACT

Smarter production
Our 40 strong team combine award-winning digital creative with cost effective technical production.

Our clients
We partner with ambitious agencies and leading brands deliver great digital products.

LONDON.
14A Shouldham St
London W1H 5FG

0044 203 384 0420

hello@athlonproduction.com

SOFIA.
13 20th April Street
1606, Sofia, Bulgaria

0035¶ 2 439 6071

ATHENS.
Agias Kiriakis 17
Kifisala 14561, Athens

0030¶ 24 39 6071

Follow 40

1.3

← → www.attackemart.in ✕

click it

hello world!

My name is Martin Gauer and
I'm a web developer from germany

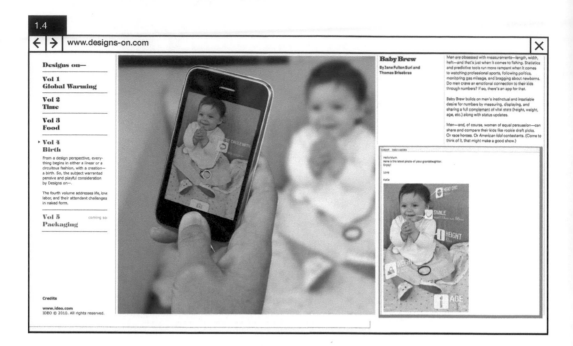

T-shaped designers

A useful metaphor to describe great designers used by the international design consultancy IDEO is 'T-shaped' designers. T-shaped designers have deep specialist knowledge of their own discipline. This enables them to be confident in explaining what they do to different specialist team members. The vertical body of a capital 'T' represents this specialist knowledge.

But deep specialist knowledge is not the end of a T-shaped designer's skill set. They also develop a secondary contextual knowledge of how other disciplines work, and a broader tertiary understanding of socio-cultural, political, ethical, ecological, economic and technological contexts. After all, design doesn't exist in a vacuum. In the T metaphor, these secondary and tertiary levels of non-specialist knowledge form the top bar of the capital T.

1.5

Breadth of knowledge

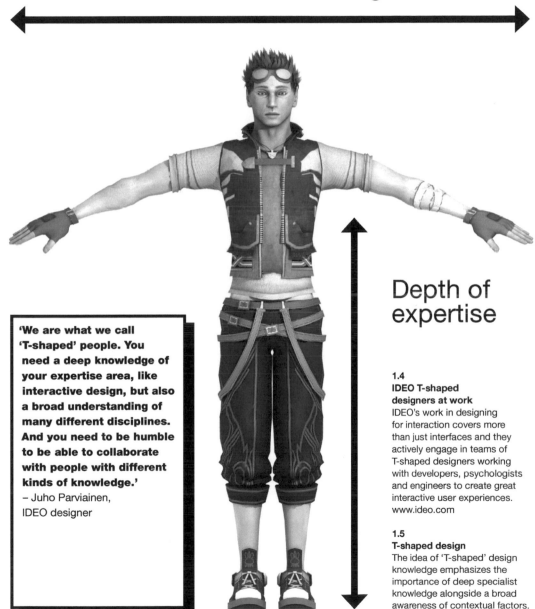

Depth of expertise

'We are what we call
'T-shaped' people. You
need a deep knowledge of
your expertise area, like
interactive design, but also
a broad understanding of
many different disciplines.
And you need to be humble
to be able to collaborate
with people with different
kinds of knowledge.'
– Juho Parviainen,
IDEO designer

1.4
**IDEO T-shaped
designers at work**
IDEO's work in designing
for interaction covers more
than just interfaces and they
actively engage in teams of
T-shaped designers working
with developers, psychologists
and engineers to create great
interactive user experiences.
www.ideo.com

1.5
T-shaped design
The idea of 'T-shaped' design
knowledge emphasizes the
importance of deep specialist
knowledge alongside a broad
awareness of contextual factors.

The scope of the graphic designer's contribution to the team throughout the design process is broad before it becomes specific. Designing for interaction is really designing the 'flow' through the interactive process in a way that creates an enjoyable and aesthetic experience for the user. Interaction itself is a loop of cause/effect/feedback, and the user experiences a flow through these steps. The UI is the visible control of that flow, and usability is the outcome of a flow designed with the user in mind.

This flow is immersive as the user doesn't always consciously realize they are in it. If the UI is well designed, the user's experience is a positive and subconscious enjoyment of the interaction. But if the UI's design causes problems, the flow is disturbed and the user is jolted out of that immersion. So to design a successful flow the following questions must be kept in mind:

— Does the user KNOW what to do in the UI?

— Can they DO what they want to do?

— Do they FEEL they have achieved something when an action is completed?

'Interaction designers answer three questions: How do you do? How do you feel? How do you know?'
– Bill Verplank, designer and researcher

1.6

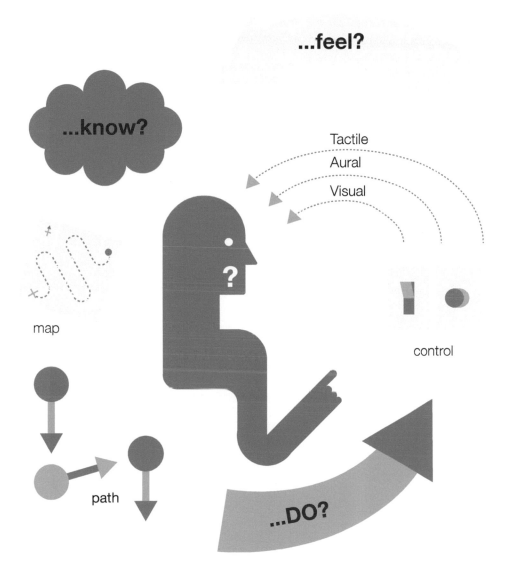

...feel?

Tactile
Aural
Visual

...know?

map

control

path

...DO?

1.6
Interaction loop
If a user knows what to do
then they also need to feel
they've achieved it. That means
a mental map, control and
feedback – a loop of interaction
(the illustration is based on a
diagram by Bill Verplank).

The graphic designer in the flow

The UI design process follows a common path, whether the project has a short or long deadline. In the existing conceptual framework of the UI design process, there is a tendency to place the graphic designer at the end of the flow under a title of 'visual design'. However, the graphic designer can make valuable contributions to the look and feel of the UI right from the beginning of a UI project. This can be in the production of personas, information architecture, wireframing and paper prototypes of the UI. They can shape the hierarchy, navigation and content, helping to identify and address visual communication problems that affect usability at an early stage, before they become too costly to correct.

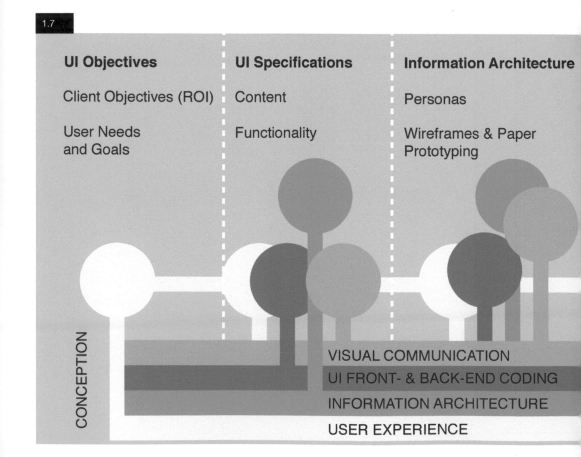

1.7

UI Objectives

Client Objectives (ROI)

User Needs
and Goals

UI Specifications

Content

Functionality

Information Architecture

Personas

Wireframes & Paper
Prototyping

CONCEPTION

VISUAL COMMUNICATION

UI FRONT- & BACK-END CODING

INFORMATION ARCHITECTURE

USER EXPERIENCE

1.7
Graphic design positioned
In this diagram, the height of the coloured circles reflects which design specialism takes the lead for that part of the process, and which are in support. This diagram demonstrates *where* graphic designers' visual communication roles *should* be utilized. As can be seen, it is *not* at the very end of the UI design process.

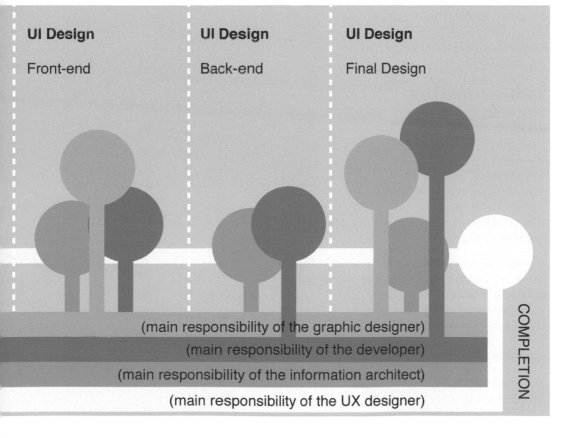

UI Design

Front-end

UI Design

Back-end

UI Design

Final Design

COMPLETION

(main responsibility of the graphic designer)
(main responsibility of the developer)
(main responsibility of the information architect)
(main responsibility of the UX designer)

We are all users. We all know the frustration we feel when an interface gives us a terrible experience, but a member of the design team is not a typical user – they know too much, preventing objectivity in UI design projects. User frustration is blamed on either themselves and/or the UI. But when the UI performs well and a user can achieve their goals with ease, the delight that ensues is attributed to the user experience. In short, a good UI is an 'invisible' UI.

The user, whether male or female, young or old, has certain personal goals when engaging with a UI. These may be to play the movie (*Blu-ray UI*), select a character (game UI), buy a book (*eCommerce UI*), or find out tomorrow's weather (*app UI*). These goals are not necessarily the same as those of the developer, the designer or even the client. The user may be the client's paying customer, but their interest is in achieving a satisfying outcome to their own interaction. It is this that the design team must make happen.

'Making the simple complicated is commonplace. Making the complicated simple, awesomely simple, that's creativity.'
– Charles Mingus

Inventory

FIGHTER

-5

Full Plate Mail Armor
Class: 1
Large Shield +1: -2
Dexterity: -4

88
112

Current Hit Points: 88
Maximum Hit Points: 112
Hit Points/Level: +4

6

Base THACO: 13
Long Sword +1 To Hit: 7

6
13

Long Sword +1: 1d8 + 1
Long Sword: +4
Number of Attacks: 2

Ground

46934

1.8

1.8
Overloading the user
The user may not be as interactive savvy as the design team. Don't overstress them with feature overload. Find out what their flow is and design for them. This ensures that the user is a constant focus in the design of the UI. In this example from *Baldur's Gate*, the use of contextual 'greyed out' calls to action indicates unavailable options at that point in the interaction.

Balancing the needs of client and user

A smooth interactive flow is the result of thorough research, implemented into clear information architecture. The client is not the actual end user. If research is based only on the client's marketing research, the resulting flow will reflect only what they would like to feature in the UI. The desires of the client and the needs of the user must be balanced so that the client gets a return on their investment (ROI), and the user is provided with a satisfying interface.

This can be achieved by conducting deeper user research, involving the user at each stage of the design process in one way or another. Focusing on designing the user's experience places design decisions within a context that forces everyone to be empathic to another human being – the user. This empathy encourages the design team and client to create a UI that helps the users achieve their individual goals.

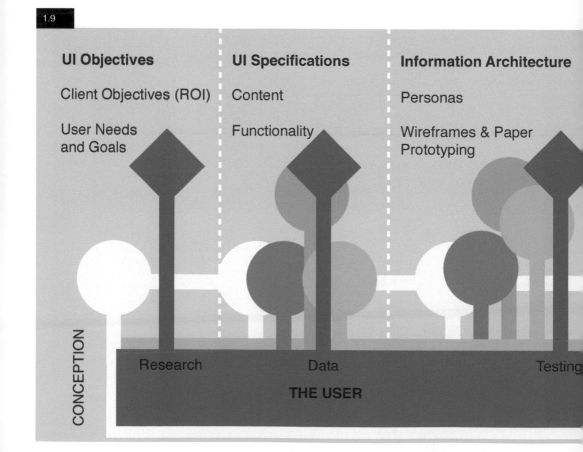

1.9

UI Objectives

Client Objectives (ROI)

User Needs and Goals

UI Specifications

Content

Functionality

Information Architecture

Personas

Wireframes & Paper Prototyping

CONCEPTION

Research   Data   Testing

THE USER

1.9
Users are king
Building upon the diagram on page 19, which demonstrated the repositioning of the graphic designer in the UI design process, this diagram focuses on where the *user* fits into the design process. Visualized in a white overlay, it is clear *where* the user 'is'. The *user* needs to be a constant focus in the design of a UI.

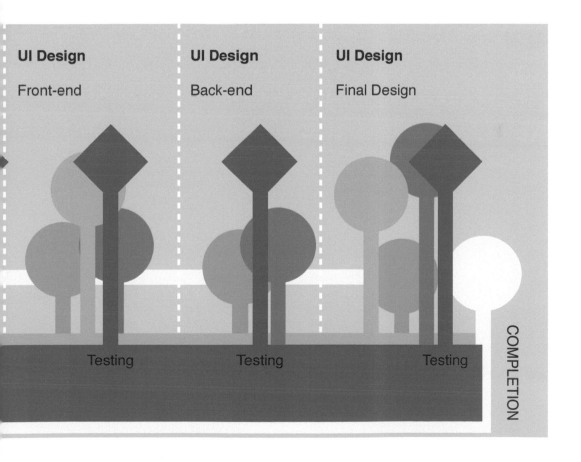

UI Design

Front-end

UI Design

Back-end

UI Design

Final Design

Testing

Testing

Testing

COMPLETION

Defining the user

The term 'user' is very generic and abstract. Marketing people have long tried to define which demographic categories consumers fit into. What age, gender, religion, sexual orientation, height, weight are we? Where do we live, shop, exercise, or work? What is our income level? These sterile facts help clients effectively target their products and services at the most relevant demographic groups, but as humans, we are more than this.

So, who is a user, in terms of UIs? They all differ in experience levels in different parts of their lives. They each have differing needs and expectations of the modes of interaction they encounter on a daily basis. Product designer Philippe Starck has a method of re-humanizing the people that his team designs for. He insists that his designers refer to them not as 'users', but with terms such as *'my friend', 'my partner', 'my mother'* or *'my father'*. By personalizing the user in this way, Starck forces his designers to instil in the otherwise abstract user a human persona. In this way, designing for their goals will be easier, as their personality can be catered for. A *user persona* embodies this.

1.10

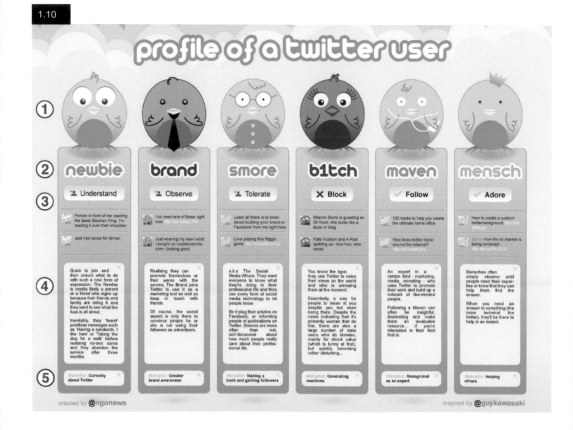

1.10

Anatomy of a profile

Ciaran Duffy, in his profiling of different types of Twitter users, creates personality archetypes featuring (1) an image, (2) name, (3) background information, (4) goals, and (5) challenges faced. These fun profiles are similar to the user information used within a persona.

1.11

Game profiles

Players of computer games will be familiar with game character profiles. To enrich the playing experience, each character has a detailed profile and backstory. It may help to think of a user persona profile like a playable game character.

1.11

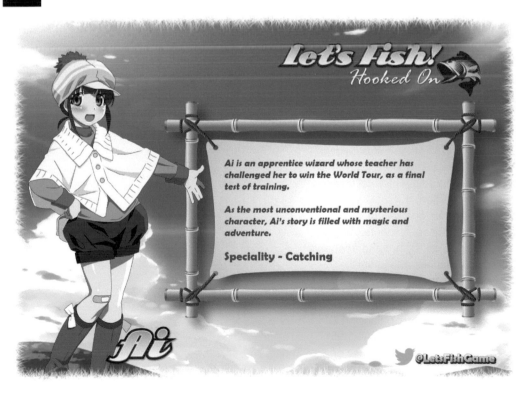

Let's Fish!
Hooked On

Ai is an apprentice wizard whose teacher has challenged her to win the World Tour, as a final test of training.

As the most unconventional and mysterious character, Ai's story is filled with magic and adventure.

Speciality - Catching

Ai

@LetsFishGame

Designing personas

A user persona is an important tool in the designer's toolkit. It is an archetype (not a stereotype) created to represent the target user(s) in a form that will inspire the design team. It takes the form of a profile with a name, an image and various amounts of information on each type of user. The creation of personas for a project really requires a graphic designer's involvement to make it valuable.

Personas are essentially a character sheet created from information gathered during research into the UI's typical users. They can be thought of as an interface between the designer and a much deeper understanding of each type of user. This approach humanizes an abstract part of the design process, helping designers to generate realistic ideas in order to drive a user to a valuable goal and understand how the UI should fulfil them. When in doubt, the design team should ask, 'What would persona A or B want at this point?'.

Persona components

Personas contain a narrative based on the user research:

A photo to personalize the persona

Name and descriptive title

Background information

Goals

Quote to summarize expectations

Breakdown of challenges faced

'The design team should ask, "What would persona A or B want at this point?".'

1.12
User persona
The use of personas at the ideation stage helps the design team identify their target audience, summarizing user motivations, expectations, experience, knowledge and desires.

1.12

Berenice Morella
UX Convert

Country: Italy
Age: 26

About Berenice
Berenice shares an apartment with two friends in Milan. She is a first year postgraduate student studying interaction design at the Domus Academy. She had worked previously as a junior graphic designer in Rome before returning to university to study user experience.

Berenice's Goals
Wants to reposition Visual Communication as a stronger influence on the design of interactions away from the misconception that she can only do the 'aesthetic bit' at the end of the project.

"I'd like to think that my design skills will help people to have more enjoyable user experiences"

Challenges
It can be tedious to analyse the results from research on the target user and she feels that there must be some tool or technique that will streamline the process.

Role
Web Usability
Consultant,
Boston, USA

Experience
Author of *Don't*
Make Me Think:
A Common Sense
Approach to
Web Usability

Web
www.sensible.com

You have said that there is a common sense element to usability. Can you explain that?

Jakob Nielsen said that usability is based on human nature. Technology changes really fast, but human nature changes really slowly. So the things that confused us ten years ago still confuse us now.

I do think that designers have become much more sophisticated about usability. Ten years ago it was very uneven, and a lot of people were still transitioning from print and hadn't gotten over it. They'd never seen a usability test. They'd never worked with anybody who had worked with user experience. There was nobody in the loop who was the user advocate. But since then, I think graphic designers have come a long way.

So I think, overall, the level of awareness that you have to have the user in mind when designing has increased fairly dramatically. It's rare that you see somebody who's just kind of completely blissfully ignorant of it. They still make all kinds of mistakes, because it is very hard to get it all right. Even sophisticated designers who have a lot of experience still make mistakes. Which is why I'm such a big advocate for doing some usability testing, no matter who you are, because there are things you're not going to be aware of until you actually watch somebody try and use it.

You mentioned that sophisticated designers still get UI design wrong. In your book you say, 'There's not a right or wrong way of doing it, but what works or doesn't work.' Can you expand on that?

I believe in being very pragmatic that way. You can implement almost any design notion. You can implement it well, or you can implement it badly.

That's the thing with interface design. Not every user is the same user. Not every interface you design is exactly the same as the last one that you've done. So this pragmatic stance is something that I think a designer needs to take on board, because you can't design the right thing all the time, can you?

Right, and what you have to keep you from having disasters is usability testing. I think you go in and you do your best shot based on your instincts. But then you've got to watch some people try and use it. That's when you find out if you've got it right or not. Other than that, you don't know.

1.13

The observer takes notes, or ideally views the test remotely via a video link.

The user will be given a task to perform using the interface.

The test equipment may be a laptop, a desktop, a TV or games console.

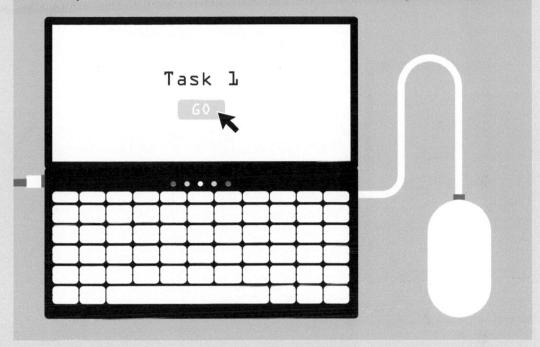

1.13
Usability testing
A simple UI usability test can be done using a laptop (or a desktop, a TV or games console) and a video camera. Steve Krug suggests testing about three or four people (not design staff) to reveal any UI problems that need addressing. Prepare a task to test the UI design, ask each user to perform that task. An observer should take notes (or, ideally, view the test remotely via a video link) and debrief the design team afterwards.

1.14

The user can be given a task to perform on a tablet or a smart phone.

Task 2

GO

Simple video camera to remotely view the touchscreen.

Camera mounted on a tripod or some other mounting.

1.14
Observation
Watching the user remotely from another room via a video link allows the design team to observe how the UI is working. User testing with a camera mounted on a tripod (or some other mounting) allows for more natural behaviour to be observed. A user can even be given a task to perform on a tablet or a smartphone and it can be observed.

If you design for people with disabilities you're obviously going to be more inclusive. Is there anything you've picked up from your workshops to get the accessibility message across to young designers?

I remember reading about students being made to put on the wrong strength reading glasses to use a website. It seemed like a pretty good approach. I do still believe the best thing you can do is to make the UI usable. Get rid of the worst problems, because if you've ever watched anyone with a disability in a usability test running into a problem that is a problem for everybody, it's like ten times worse for them.

In chapter 2 of this book I discuss hierarchy, wireframes and paper prototyping. Within usability testing, what's your opinion on paper prototyping your early UI designs, before any code or branding has been applied?

Well, it's a great thing to do. It works really well, and the thing I always tell people is they can test anything. But the truth is that there's not a whole lot you can test with wireframes. You can test the navigation, you can test some of your hierarchy and that kind of thing, but it's not going to get very far. But with the roughest paper prototype you can. It's hard to get people to do it though, unless they've seen it done and had experience with it.

Would you say that a good interface is essentially something that would become 'invisible' because the user experience allows people to effortlessly get what they want from the UI?

In many cases if you're using a thing and you're not aware of it having an interface, then it probably means the interface has been tuned so well that it is meeting your expectations constantly. That's why you're not aware of it – because it's meeting your expectations. So obviously that's a really good thing. It can be as great looking as you want to make it as long as the looks don't get in the way of the user doing what they want to do. I'm very much in favour of stylishly designed apps.

Is there any advice you would give directly to a designer, as opposed to advice to a developer?

Hard as it may be to treat all these people as your friends, try and find a way to respect what the rest of the design team does. It may not look like it to you, but their job is just as hard as yours. They're scared and intimidated at the start of each new project – even though they may not look it. Developers are just as scared as designers; and project managers are just as scared as developers.

Project
www.
weprintpaper.
co.uk

Design team
**elloDave,
Staffordshire, UK**

Client
We Print Paper

The project

elloDave is a young creative agency based in the UK, with a focus on designing online and printed marketing campaigns. This extends to designing web presences, especially for new start-up businesses. One such company, We Print Paper, wanted help developing a website through which they could sell their affordable, online automated printing services. As the client was a start-up, elloDave had the benefit of a flexible deadline lasting over six months.

Among elloDave's staff was final year graphic design student Ben Pritchard, who took on responsibility for the design and art direction of the website as an employed designer. Ben conducted research, exploring what the client's competitors provided and what visitors to the website would actually want. It became clear to elloDave that the client's order process was a unique selling point to the user, which could be subtly exploited in the client's favour.

Ben's research also revealed that the customer base would be tech-savvy people with digital artwork ready to print online. This understanding provided clear user needs and goals to design for.

1.15
Original ideas
When Ben began working at elloDave, the website's original design wasn't working for the client. He began a total redesign of the entire website from the ground up. The final design of the website took six design iterations. The first iteration of the redesign began by giving the interface clearly defined horizontal content areas, and removing the candy-coloured icons in favour of a more subtle approach.

1.16
Third version comp
Ben, through each of his design iterations, composited the UI design together in Adobe Photoshop and Illustrator ready to be converted into CSS3. He labelled each element's layer so that it could seamlessly be exported for the developer to use in the code.

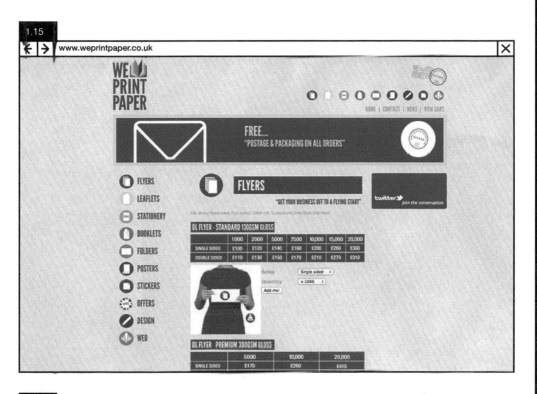

1.15

www.weprintpaper.co.uk

1.16

1.17
Final version: Illustrator rough
The design of the final UI aesthetic was first compiled in Illustrator. The UI elements were aligned to a grid, with the accuracy that the vector program can give.

1.18
Final version:
Photoshop comp
Finally, the design was transferred into Photoshop to separate into modular UI components. These were set pixel-perfect, and labelled ready for coding.

1.17

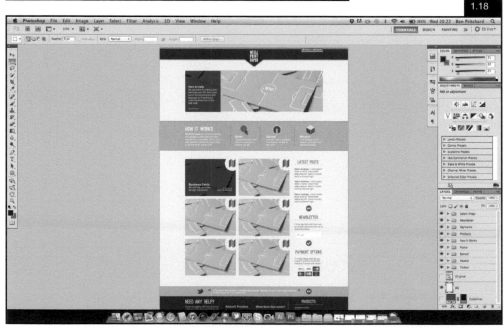

1.18

The graphic designer's contribution

Through early planning meetings, the design team explored and defined the site's information architecture (IA). From the IA, they checked which designs would and wouldn't work for the user, and what the client needed as a return on their investment. They then agreed the technical and aesthetic requirements that would be needed to make the best user experience, and therefore sell the client's product and service. Originally, the website was to be coded in-house. But with the order process being the main user-centred function behind the client's business model, more specialist help was needed from a freelance developer.

Working hand-in-hand with the developer, Ben collaborated on shaping the aesthetic and code to create the desired user experience. Through continued dialogue, the graphic designer and developer found different ways to design the aesthetic and push the code. Using HTML, CSS markup and server-side programming, the developer connected the file uploader to a back-end ordering system.

A T-shaped Ben

The project took six months. In that time the user experience went through six iterations before elloDave were satisfied. The decisions Ben made on the visual communication gave visual affordances (clues or signposts) to the developer's code. A suitably restricted colour palette emerged to subtly appeal to the client's customers.

By working closely with the developer, Ben broke his final designs down into component parts ready for the developer to code. Some parts of the design would be images (labelled for the developer), others would be visualized in the code via CSS.

Ben clearly demonstrated his development into a 'T-shaped' designer during this project (see page 15). He began the project as a final year undergraduate design student, working as a professional graphic designer for elloDave on day release. Through engaging with each team member during the project, he learned exactly what a graphic designer can contribute to a complex design project.

Finding the flow: Designing interaction

We have seen how the design of a successful interface is a complex iterative process, and that visual communication is an important part of it. To illustrate how the designer's role contributes to interface design, the subjects of information architecture, navigation, wireframes and paper prototyping will be discussed in this chapter. These all take place during the early ideation and scoping phases of designing interfaces, before any branding has begun.

This chapter will take you beneath the surface of the graphical user interface (GUI) to reveal how to design the flow of interactivity.

Humans were not programmed for computer use. Therefore computers (in all their many guises) have to be programmed to deal with humans, and it is the UI that enables interaction between the two. It is the UI that makes the interaction more intuitive, through direct input and immediate feedback. In screen-based media, the UI is referred to as a graphical user interface (GUI). GUIs create visual affordances ('clues' to the purpose of particular elements within a design) through the graphic design, which communicate the navigation, the interaction and the content in an interface through the use of visual metaphor. Traditionally, GUIs have been designed with WIMPs – windows, icons, menus and a pointer. Through these visual components the user can interact and achieve their desired outcomes. GUIs now also take a variety of post-WIMP forms across a variety of digital, screen-based media.

Windows, icons, menus, pointer (WIMP)

We are familiar with WIMP GUIs in the software we use every day in our personal and professional lives (such as Adobe InDesign, Illustrator and Photoshop). We are used to the working metaphors of opening computer windows on our desktop, selecting menu options with a cursor pointer, and clicking on icons to perform tasks on our personal computers, DVDs, TVs and in computer games. GUIs can be found on the Web, accessed through browsers. They are on our TVs in cable/satellite channel programme guides, on our DVD and Blu-ray (BD) players, video game consoles, and in our hands with portable media devices. A WIMP GUI relies on input predominantly controlled by a computer mouse. Alternative input devices for WIMP GUIs also include a stylus, a remote control, a game controller/joystick/steering wheel or a trackpad on a laptop.

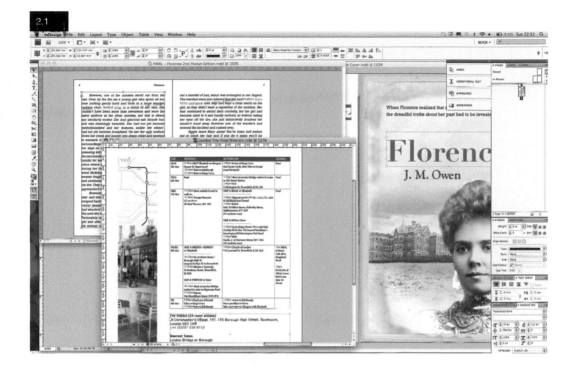

2.1
WIMP

Windows, icons, menus and pointers (WIMP) GUIs rely on input devices, such as a mouse, to make selections from menus and icons using the mouse's cursor as a pointer. The content is displayed in windows. WIMPs are visual affordances for users to interact with the computer. Although not as quick as command lines, these GUIs are much easier to use for those of us who are not computer scientists.

Post-WIMP

The personal computer is no longer bound to the desktop. The GUI is also on our smartphones, tablets and now the interaction is inputted in a more tactile and direct way. We are now in a post-WIMP world where input through a GUI to access content has become much more direct. The inputs of post-WIMP interfaces have moved beyond a mouse's pointer, allowing us to navigate windows, select menus and click icons through touch and gestures. This means that the designer can no longer rely on just designing a variation on a metaphorical WIMP interface solution. The design team needs to design for the user experience in new and exciting ways, where the *user* is the input controller.

Interaction using post-WIMP GUIs in these new apps and digital devices happens through both tactile (finger/thumb tips) and gestural (hand/body movements) sensory inputs. To successfully design for this form of interaction, the design team needs to understand the:

— psychology of the user and their requirements

— technology to be used

— desires of the client and their stakeholders

2.2

2.2
Touch interaction
Within a post-WIMP interface
the design of the interactions
must consider a more direct
input to access the content via
touch.

2.3
Kinect-embodied interaction
Post-WIMP interface design
also needs to incorporate
embodied interaction.

An integral part of designing for interaction is to first understand which elements need to interact with each other. Therefore it is important to know what the content will be, who it is aimed at and what technology it will be available on.

Whichever form and media the interface takes, whether it is a website, DVD, mobile app or a game interface, interaction flow needs to be revealed and structured. By understanding what needs to be connected through a GUI, the optimum interactive structure can be devised. The responsibility for this mainly falls on the shoulders of an information architect, in consultation with the design team. On behalf of the design team, the information architect designs a navigation pathway through the UI's content. The resulting interactive structure and navigation pathway is referred to as the information architecture (IA). This informs the functional form a graphical UI will take, from which the designer and developer conceptualize the most effective aesthetic user experience.

Functionality and usability

Information architecture follows a process of research, analysis and evaluation to communicate to the UI design team how the target users will obtain their goals. It ensures the interactive structure reflects an appropriate user experience. It is not enough to have functionality; that functionality needs to work for the person using it in a way that makes sense to them.

The IA focuses on making the UI structure usable, and this is of primary importance to the user. Usability begins when design facilitates the user's goals. This builds a user's confidence and raises their comfort level. In turn, the client can capitalize on a positive user experience by converting this user satisfaction into sales or leads.

Information architecture, just like traditional building architecture, comes before anything is built. By the same token, graphic design also comes before the finished build. Graphic designers can contribute to the production of the IA alongside an information architect. But what does an information architect actually do?

2.4

2.4
Navigation pathway
Information architecture reveals
an optimum navigation pathway
through the content to ensure
goals are met prior to creating a
UI roadmap diagram.

Ease of use

Users of all abilities fail interactive tests
that are confusing. Too often, design teams
overestimate the amount of complexity
that users can easily handle. They also
underestimate the extent to which using a
new interface can be a strain and barrier to
learning. This is compounded if design teams
assume all users are equally capable. Attention
to UI accessibility issues early on, through
research and testing, will reach more users
with or without disabilities. This will make the
UI more successfully effortless to use.

The architect of flow

Information architecture helps the graphic designer, the developer and the design team comprehend the breadth and depth of the interactivity that the UI needs to facilitate. The IA maps a flow through the content before any design or code has been created.

An information architect's role consists of several tasks: creating a content inventory, defining user personas, revealing the interactive flow and hierarchy, creating a UI roadmap diagram, and labelling all the relevant parts with 'user-facing' names.

The architect first examines the client's 'as-is' status (their current position) and their 'to-be' status (the new position the UI intends to occupy). This exposes any content gaps, dependencies, or content changes, allowing the architect to assess how far the client's desired position is from their current position. This gap analysis suggests a business strategy within which the UI will exist; the desired goals that the users of the UI will expect; and how the UI will make a return on the client's investment (ROI).

An example to explain this is suggested by UX designer Kristin Kramer. If a stationery supply company uses an e-commerce website to sell printers, the company's 'to-be' position would reflect their need to sell more printers through their UI. So as the design team's client, the stationery company would want to feature printer X on the website's homepage, because they think that it is 'at the right price' for their customers. But the customer (user) is not just concerned about the price – they might care more about colour reproduction. The information architect will appreciate this and will ensure that both these pieces of information are clearly communicated by finding the intersection of client (want to sell printer) and customer/user (want to buy printer).

The architect will understand these conflicts and prioritize a flow solution based on user behaviour. This solution is based on research that is gathered to understand both the audience and the client's needs. The main outcome of IA is a diagram of these relationships between content areas. This diagram has many alternative names, such as site map, site hierarchy map, site diagram, blueprint, or web map. The term we'll use throughout this book is 'UI roadmap'.

2.5

Visualization tools

The software from Microsoft, Omnigroup, Assure and Adobe all do similar things: draw boxes and links between boxes. Software is useful to cleanly visualize the relationships between content areas; but pens, string, paper and a wall do exactly the same thing. Some favoured IA software includes:

— Microsoft Visio

— Omnigroup OmniGraffle

— Assure Axure

— Adobe Illustrator

— Pens, sticky notes, string and a wall

2.5
Communication tools
The clear communication of important content will be managed by an information architect to ensure that the important content is accessible and that flow is maintained. This can be achieved with software such as Vision or OmniGraffle – or with low-tech pen and paper.

The IA reveals complexity of relationships between content, and how the navigation needs to work. There are two forms that navigation takes: global and contextual.

Global navigation is available from every page of the UI. Examples include links to the homepage, to help, to print, and so on. Contextual navigation may only be available in a particular area of the UI, or on a particular subject page. An example of this would be the options on each window of a software installation where the buttons change their action-calls depending on what step of the process has been reached. Good global navigation allows the possibility of transporting the user across the UI structure to content of their choice in a non-linear way. Contextual navigation, on the other hand, allows exploration within specifically associated content.

Mapping the UI

A UI roadmap diagram allows the design team to instantly see the content and navigation hierarchy and all 'parent/child' relationships between associated content areas. It also shows whether the navigation is linear (screen following screen consecutively) or non-linear (jumping from screen to screen in any order that the user chooses). This will show where global or contextual navigation is required, and what needs to link to what.

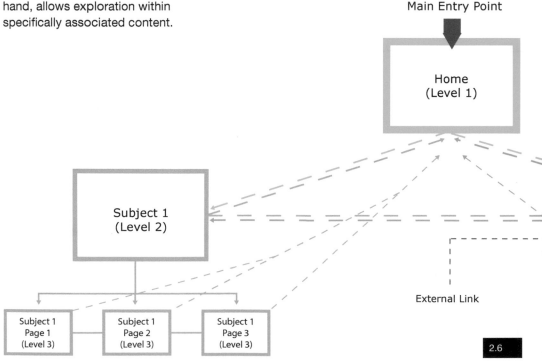

2.6

The layout of the IA as a diagram can be shown in a variety of ways. Two common methods are to use a hierarchical gridded structure, showing each level in neat rows, or to use a navigation contextual structure, showing associations. Either way, the IA content hierarchy will show the levels of association, which can be summarized as (1) main level, (2) subject groupings, and (3) subject group sub-content.

This content hierarchy mirrors similar thought processes that a graphic designer considers when designing a visual hierarchy for the UI. It is essential for a graphic designer to understand the IA process, as they can then appreciate the rationale behind the interactive structure.

2.6
Website and DVD
Information architecture is not just for the Web, it's for any interface, such as an app, a game, a DVD or Blu-ray.

— Level 1
Level 1 of the interaction includes the main entry point and immediate subject areas. Dotted lines indicate navigation and boxes indicate screens.

— Level 2
The subject areas are often on the second level of interaction.

— Level 3
The third level of content is often the specific content within each subject area. Therefore, Level 3 offers clear areas for subject-specific content. In non-linear navigation, the connections between levels are quite complex and need to be visually communicated simply through the interface design to hide the complexity.

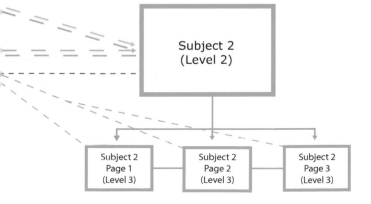

The user needs to be able to differentiate navigation from content and all the interactive options available to them. A hierarchical structure is used to separate all the UI's distinct and group-related elements. This begins with defining a visual hierarchy of important UI elements – from high importance, to secondary and then tertiary importance. Consistency is crucial in achieving this. But context also has an important part to play. The visual hierarchy of headers, navigation and content is contextual and layered depending on which page or section of content the user is currently in. A hierarchy affords the user an effortless flow through the interface by communicating what is accessible, what is interactive, and what to do next.

Therefore, every visual element that is designed for the UI should be there to reveal important information. Any elements that are given greater prominence should be doing that for a reason, otherwise user confusion and frustration ensues.

There are standards and conventions to structuring the visual hierarchy that should be followed. This still allows a designer plenty of scope for design innovation if they consult their user research and the user personas to support their design decisions. If the personas suggest a conservative user, then conventional standards should be followed. But if the personas reveal otherwise, the designer has an opportunity to innovate a more exciting user experience, while still ensuring the user can achieve their goals.

Interface hierarchies

Graphic designers have a rich visual language that has been developed over the last century through design for print. Since the advent of the Web in the 1990s, this visual language has been adapted to embrace interactivity. An interface should be usable, and graphic designers – with a solid training in visual communication – understand that visual hierarchy helps reduce any miscommunication 'noise'.

Hierarchy helps communicate important information about interface navigation so that the user knows when navigation is global, and when it is only available within a specific context.

2.7
UI hierarchy 1
This is a visual hierarchy within a selection screen from the game *Sim City*:
(1) Screen title.
(2) Global navigation.
(3) Contextual navigation.
(4) Main content.
(5) Contextual content.
(6) Contextual information.

2.8
UI hierarchy 2
The hierarchy of navigational content within a limited screen space needs to also focus on the principal goals a user will want to achieve. But within limited screen space locations will vary from a desktop version:
(1) Screen title.
(2) Global navigation.
(3) Contextual navigation.
(4) Main content.
(5) Contextual content.
(6) Contextual information.

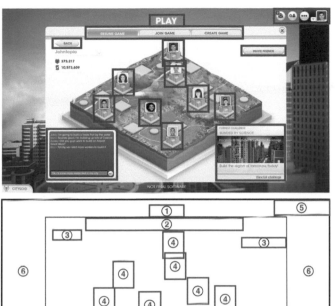

2.7

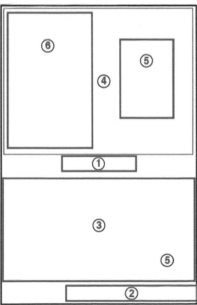

2.8

Clarity through graphic design

The underlying hierarchical scaffold a designer uses to structure the visual elements is a grid structure. With grids come decisions on formal (highly structured) or informal (more fluid) composition of visual elements. The graphic designer will manipulate and balance these elements using symmetry, visual rhythm and frequency of repetition to help the user to understand what is being indicated as their next possible step.

This manipulation and balancing is reliant on visual weighting, allowing the eye to pass over and pause on important visual elements. Patterns, colour and textures can help identify changes in content areas. The balance of spacing and proximity of elements, the variance of line, shape, image, typography and form all help to avoid visual clutter. This crafting of the visual communication by the graphic designer creates unhindered movement and paths through the content. By building a visual hierarchy on an underlying grid, the user can be guided to those parts of the current UI screen that they are looking for.

The use of a visual hierarchy acknowledges that part of the design process is designing a positive emotional response in the user to the UI. If the interface is designed well, users will attribute their sense of delight with using the UI to a satisfying user experience. But any frustration with the UI will be blamed on the design of the interface itself. If designers have done a good job, then their interface will be invisible to the user. An invisible interface is an interface that attracts and retains user attention, with the aesthetic and functionality working harmoniously together.

athome.nfb.ca/#/athome/home

WINNIPEG

MONTREAL

ADDED 05.05.12

A MODEL PERSON
MR. MADDOGG, HOUSED PARTICIPANT

VANCOUVER

TORONTO

MONCTON

THE BLOG

THE BACKSTORY   2 DAYS LEFT   29 FILMS TO COME   THE EXPERIMENT

HOME | INTRO | ALL FILMS | ABOUT THE WEBDOC | RELATED FILMS | CREDITS   ◎ SHARE | ▲ MUTE | ⤢ FULLSCREEN

2.9
Every element
Every visual element placed on
a UI screen should be there for
a reason. Even in this dynamic
data-driven UI from a website
by The National Film Board of
Canada the visual hierarchy
remains clear: the user knows
the title, the navigation and
the content, while the site still
retains a playful edge.

There is a great deal of research into human-computer interaction, in terms of what works in an interface design and what does not.

People think 'top-down', so to enhance interactivity you should make navigation obvious, convenient and easy to use. The labelling of navigation should use succinct 'user-facing' terms that they will understand. This will ensure that users have a logical path to follow through the UI. On smaller screens and tablets, the navigational information hierarchy should be restrained. To implement these conventions, it is important to test the design solutions early and often.

Testing the navigation

Whether the interface is for a website, an app, a BD (Blu-ray disc) or video game, navigation usually takes the form of tabs, menus, buttons, or hypertext links. Tabs and menus have come to indicate the navigation locations, while buttons and links indicate action. This helps the user to understand where they are within the interactive structure, and know where they can proceed to next.

If the user has no idea how to use the navigation, they will leave the UI in frustration. So testing is crucial, and that means testing the proposed UI design with 'real' users – not the design team. It is important that testing is conducted early – even at the ideation stage before any branding or coding has been done.

Examples of UI design guidelines all available in the public domain:

— GEL (Global Experience Language) the BBC's web UI guidelines for designing their interactive services
www.bbc.co.uk/gel

— Mozilla's Brand Toolkit for open source developers of the Firefox browser
www.mozilla.org/en-US/styleguide

— Apple's Human Interface Guidelines for iPhone, iPad and MAC OS interfaces
developer.apple.com

— Alertbox website – Usability expert Jakob Nielsen's website on web usability
www.nngroup.com/articles

2.10

iPhone Wireframe Template

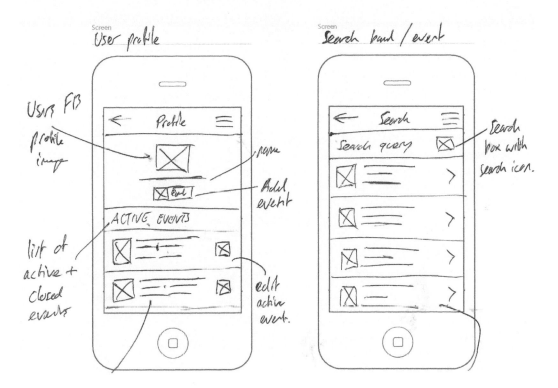

Screen
User profile

Usrs FB
profile
image

Profile

name

Add
event

ACTIVE EVENTS

list of
active +
closed
events

edit
active
event.

Screen
Search band / event

Search

Search query

Search
box with
search icon.

2.10
Vote Band wireframes
Global and contextual
navigational flow to content are
clearly indicated in these early
wireframe diagrams for the
VoteBand™ app. The flow from
one area to the next is indicated
by the handwritten annotations
(wireframes will be discussed in
the next section).

Wireframing

Wireframes are a useful tool with which to test the design team's assumptions early in the design phase. They reveal the underlying logic, behaviour and functionality of each UI screen. The information architecture will have shown the designer what content goes where and what needs to link to what. This information needs to ultimately become a usable, intuitive interface. But how can this be communicated to the user visually? This lies within the skill of the graphic designer, in collaboration with the design team.

The wireframe is not the finished UI design; it is a method for deciding what will need to be included. It takes the IA and considers the technical platforms that the UI will be accessed from. The wireframe also considers the input from the user (finger, thumb, mouse or gestural). In itself, a wireframe is simply a proposed layout using nothing more than lines, boxes and basic text. In this very basic way it can show possible frameworks for the visual hierarchy, navigation priorities and suitable content areas.

Wireframes show only boxes and minimal text devoid of any aesthetic or code, just to give a feel for what the UI needs to feature. As such, wireframing has been seen as primarily an information architect's task, but the team's graphic designer should certainly advise as early as possible on the visual communication aspects of a wireframe. This will balance the advice on the coding and user experience requirements, and won't restrict later design phases.

Wireframing all the important UI screens is crucial to communicate possible solutions, referring back to the personas (see page 27) when decisions need to be agreed. Sketched at full-pixel scale for the digital media it will be used on, a wireframe can be tested very quickly with real users in a very informal conversation. This is a quick and positive way to test the functionality of the UI so that the visual communication of it can be optimized.

Although the aesthetic is absent from a wireframe, it is still important to indicate in full scale the location of headers, footers, sidebars, navigation, content areas, and secondary links. This highlights the number of variations and reusable elements that would be needed in the final design.

Wireframes do not work when:

— they are confused with a finished design – keep them as outlines with no branding.

— they dictate an absolute layout to a designer – wireframes should still be flexible.

— a graphic designer is not engaged in a wireframe design – involve a designer.

2.11
Wireframe development
Wireframes are not the final design that just needs 'colouring in'. It is an active dialogue that will guide the designer in their design iterations. When user flow is understood, a designer in consultation with the information architect can help sketch a wireframe of all that needs to feature on each interface screen. This shows the scope of the elements that need to be included in the final graphic design for the interface.

Paper prototyping

Paper prototyping adds another dimension to what wireframing achieves. Based on the wireframe outlines, whole sections of the UI can be quickly tested for functionality, revealing any design problems.

The paper prototype is not meant to test the code or any visual communication beyond the basic interactive structure. The UI is sketched on paper – again without any branding or identity (only navigation labels and headers will be written in full). Lines of scribbles are drawn to indicate where body text will go, boxes with crosses indicate images or video.

This rough 'low-fidelity' (lo-fi) paper prototype focuses the user's feedback on the UI's functionality and interactive flow. To ensure it presents enough to test, all the main UI parts need to be drawn, such as variants of screens and elements. Users are presented with the first paper 'screen' and will be given a task to achieve. Testing around a given task in this way generates questions that demand solutions.

The testing of a paper prototype proceeds one sheet of paper at a time, with each sheet representing a window, menu, action and so on. The user will use their finger to point to 'click' where they believe links to be. With each click, the paper screen is changed to represent the next interactive step. Any additional elements, or changes needed to existing ones, can quickly be made to the paper prototype, often right in front of the user testing it.

Testing during this early design phase generates valuable communication and synergy between the design team, client and intended users. Any problem solving comes from this observation of each user and helps a designer understand user thought processes. Testing a proposed UI solution in such a lo-fi way is a valuable and cost-efficient way to convince a client of the validity of the final design solution.

To get the most out of the test, it is important that the design team only observes and lets the user dictate their flow through the interface. If possible, the design team should use video cameras to observe the user from a distance, so they do not unintentionally influence them.

2.12

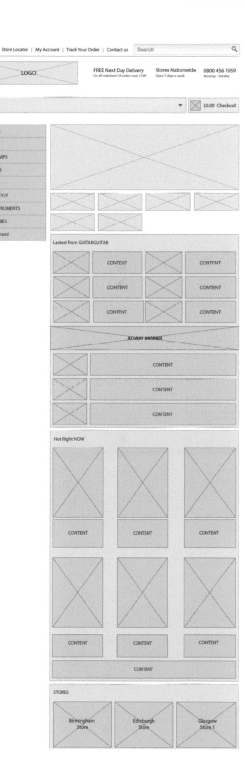

2.12

Hi-fi wireframing

Once the wireframing dialogue
in the team has happened, and
consensus has been reached
as to the optimum layout that
will help the user achieve
their goals, a more polished
wireframe can be produced to
ensure clarity of communication.

Role
Honours
undergraduate
student, Glasgow,
Scotland, UK

Experience
BA(Hons) Graphic
Design for
Digital Media

Web
www.greggibson.
co.uk

As an undergraduate student working on your Honours project you're exploring website visual hierarchy. What is it about web hierarchy that is useful to you as a graphic design student?

Well, the reason I chose visual hierarchy is to see how to guide the user around an interface using visual elements. I think I began to delve into it when I was on exchange in Finland and learning about the theories of Jakob Nielsen and Steve Krug. I always knew I wanted to do web design. I really wanted to find out what these theories really mean.

I have categorized the hierarchy into three different visual elements: colour, layout and typography. Different typefaces you can use obviously give a tone of voice for the website. A sans serif could be used for titles and then a serif for the content areas. Colour is used to link important areas. In layout, especially in Western cultures, we read left to right. So the most important area is the top left, and the least important the bottom right. There are a lot of technical aspects about layout within web design. When you're coding you have to lay out the content so that it will work in different browsers.

The way people interact with the Internet now is with mobile phones and tablets, so you have to really consider layout for all these devices. I think that is the main difference between the layout of print and web. It's mainly to do with the coding and that you have to consider using percentages now.

So you saw the relevance between traditional print-based graphic design techniques and applying it for the Web?

Yeah. The grid has been around for ages. But the Web is new, and constantly advancing so I was able to just adapt it to this new medium.

So far in your Honours project you began by looking at wireframing to understand interactive structure. Why did you think it was important to do that?

I had to design a website for a client in another degree module. The first stage of this meant analysing websites that were similar to what the client was proposing, which was an architectural website. So I looked into seven or eight different websites to understand how they laid out the content, why they did it that way and find the most interesting examples. I did that using wireframes to really break down the content without the distraction of actual images. That then led me on to a layout for my own website design. It improved the overall website and how the user would interact with it. The feedback from the client was really good.

With laying out the content, I could quickly see where things were wrong, and didn't look good, or a user couldn't interact with it. I printed out screenshots of each site, and put tracing paper over it and drew each bit. I boxed out all the navigation, the main content areas, and then tried to figure out what sort of grid system they used. It's surprising how many people don't really think about it. But when designers do actually use a grid system, you can work it out and see how they laid out the content. I guess it proved that the grid system made things look consistent, but there was also room for variation.

Have you looked into making the website dynamic to scale across any browser, on any platform, on any machine?

Yes. I think what they do in the coding is use percentages so the content can fluctuate, but they also have different stylesheets for different platforms. So if you are using it on a mobile device, it will change to a different layout. Only a certain amount of information will be displayed on the small screen compared to a laptop.

From an early stage you've had an interest in eye-tracking usability tests. What was it about that particular type of usability test that appealed to you?

When you're showing a design to a client who does not have a graphic design background, they do not really understand the layout of the content. So eye-tracking tests (see page 61) is a way of proving the methods, and giving the client facts and figures that they can understand. I can show them that if they do the design one way it won't work, but if they do it another way it will. Having the physical evidence is one of the main things I want to achieve.

So how many people do you think you will need to test?

I'm thinking about five to six people will be enough to have a variation on how people interact with it. I'll revise the design using the results and hopefully come up with an even better design. I'll then have the results to show why I have implemented the design in that sort of way. I'll then redo it and see if the users interact with it in a better way, and are more satisfied with it. I think with design you're always learning, especially in web design. You always have to keep pushing yourself.

Project
Hats or icons
www.vedderprice.
com/london/

Design team
Fishman
Marketing Inc.,
Illinois, USA

Client
Vedder Price LLP,
London, UK

Finding the flow

In a recent marketing campaign for the Chicago-based law firm Vedder Price's new London office, Fishman Marketing used eye-tracking technology to test two shortlisted website designs. Eye-tracking uses cameras to trace a user's eye movements around a screen. The data it generates can be used to determine how effective a website's visual hierarchy is.

The two designs, 'Hats' and 'Icons', were intended to help Vedder Price's new London office convey the same strategic message – that they're supporting their aviation finance practice from London, UK. The company had a complex target audience who would require different information and amounts of detail from the website. It was important for the website design to communicate an aviation- and London-focused identity to this audience, and generate income for Vedder Price's new UK-based office.

2.13
Hats and Icons
The two website ideas were 'Hats' (left) and 'Icons' (right). The former was a humorous design based around iconic British hats, and the latter was deemed more conservative, focusing on comparative icons from the USA and the UK.

2.14
Eye tracking
The eye-tracking software follows the user's eyes around the UI screen to see what areas they look at the most. These areas show up the hottest (red).

2.15
Viewing order
The eye tracking is useful in establishing the order in which the visual hierarchy is actually viewed. This information is useful for a designer in evaluating their design decisions regarding the UI's aesthetic.

2.13

Visual attention level

More attention   Less attention

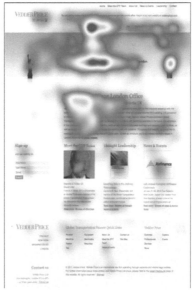

Fixation order*

*based on average time to first fixation

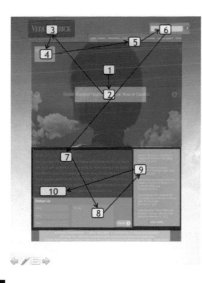 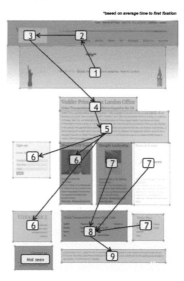

Testing the flow

Eye-tracking software generates data, rather than opinions, from a test audience. It helps the design team examine the order in which the users viewed the content, and for how long. The flow of each user's attention through the visual hierarchy is recorded via cameras, tracking eye movements around the screen. These eye movements create 'hotspots' on the screen, indicating the areas users looked at the most and for the longest period of time. This collected data works on a principle that users often 'scan' content rather than reading it, and such testing helps quantify the areas they spend the most time on.

Evaluating the flow

Results from the eye-tracking testing showed that the more conservative 'Icons' design idea proved more successful to the intended audience than the 'Hats' idea. Although two thirds of those tested thought the 'Hats' idea was more creative, the aesthetic style was deemed not to be as effective as the more traditional 'Icons' idea. As the target audience was international, and needed to be comfortable with the new office's London-focused website, the 'Icons' design was chosen.

The user testers received both ideas positively, but the 'Icons' idea recorded 96 per cent of users noticing the important headline 'Vedder Price's New London Office.' They spent 2.5 seconds reading it, and then spent 4 seconds scanning the supporting news paragraph. On 'Icons', this was the fourth thing that users found, whilst it was the seventh thing that was looked at on the 'Hats' design. The use of eye tracking helped confirm that the 'Icons' website design conveyed Vedder Price's message more effectively to its target audience.

> **'Great UI design doesn't just make something attractive. It makes it effective.'**
> – Ross Fishman,
> Fishman Marketing

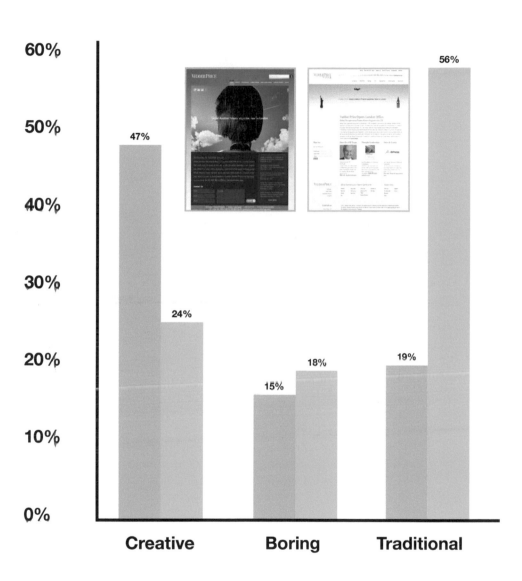

60%	
	56%
50%	
47%	
40%	
30%	
24%	
20%	18% 19%
15%	
10%	
0%	
Creative	Boring Traditional

2.16
Quantitative summary
This bar chart quantitatively
summarizes the data from
the user tests, demonstrating
perception calls on which
design was qualitatively
more effective.

2.16

2.17

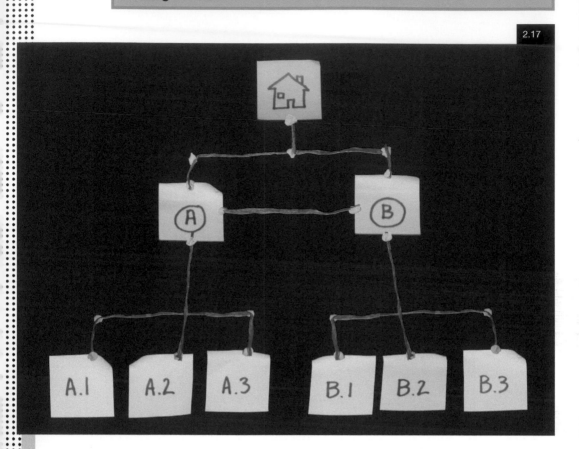

2.17
The final outcome
You should end up with something like this, showing specific content sections (colour-coded sticky notes), and demonstrating parent/child relationships between the section main page and its own content pages. In your version (A), (B) etc will be replaced with the links on the homepage. A.1, B.1 etc will be replaced with the links on each subject page.

Premise

In this chapter, information architecture and hierarchy (of navigation, content and the visual) have been discussed. Understanding underlying interactive structure is important to the design of a successful UI. But where does this understanding begin?

This exercise will allow you to understand flow by deconstructing an existing interface. What you learn can inspire and inform you in any future UI design projects. You can conduct this task on your own or in groups, and it only requires four things:

— sticky notes in several colours

— string (different coloured cotton, wool or twine would be fine)

— Blu Tack (or any reusable wall display putty)

— a big wall.

Exercise

1 Choose an existing small UI.

2 Write 'Homepage' on a colour sticky note and place it centrally on the wall. This is level 1.

3 Write on a different colour sticky note, each section/subject name that appears on the homepage ('About', 'Contact', etc). Place these in a row underneath the 'Homepage' note. The colour change indicates that these pages are at level 2.

4 Using the string and wall putty, connect the 'Homepage' to the level 2 subject pages.

5 Now focusing on each subject page separately, look at what links are in that section (for example, the 'About' section pages may feature pages on 'History,' 'Team', etc). Use a smaller sticky note to record these sub-pages that form level 3.

6 Stick these smaller sticky notes on the wall under their 'parent' section, grouping them under their subject to show association and context.

7 Using string, connect these smaller sticky notes to each other and to their parent.

8 After repeating steps 5, 6 and 7 for each section/subject area, use a different colour string to connect each page BACK to the homepage, AND to any other page that is linked.

Note: For this exercise, stop at LEVEL 3, even if the chosen website has more levels.

Outcomes

You should see a very rough hierarchy of interactions on the wall across the three content levels. Is the revealed interactive structure far more complex than you initially thought it would be? This technique works for any form of UI (BD/DVD, app, even game UI). It makes you deconstruct the complex flow of how content is made accessible to the user.

Graphic design for digital media

This chapter discusses the important building blocks of graphic design for digital media, which are crucial for creating effective visual communication within a UI. Grids, typography, colour, images, motion, iconography and metaphor are explained and put into a context that can be applied to the design of any UI.

Interactivity, technological platforms and the display screen are all important factors that the graphic designer must consider. These factors provide both constraints and opportunities for design innovation.

A grid is an underlying framework that graphic designers use to place content and navigation in a controlled way, to aid visual communication and define a focal point on the UI screen.

Within UI design there has always been an issue regarding set sizes to design for. In print design, set page sizes such as A4, A3 or US Letter are clear, but with digital devices and different screen resolutions there are far more variants to consider. Screen resolution needs to be taken into account as it dictates how many pixels are available in the grid. Therefore, a UI graphic designer needs to understand how grids can help them design better BD/DVD, game, web, TV, tablet or smartphone interfaces.

3.1
Resolution guide
It is crucial when designing a UI that the design team has a clear understanding of what resolutions are available to them, so they can design in confidence that the user will have the UI optimized for their display.

3.2
The Grid System
The use of an underlying grid allows designers to establish a clear, effective hierarchy and thereby allows content to be clearly accessed. The Grid System is a very helpful resource, explaining more about how to choose and use a grid in your designs.
www.thegridsystem.org

Grids – functioning aesthetics

A grid consists of both vertical and horizontal sections forming columns, rows, margins and gutters. The baseline of the grid is informed by the x-height of the typeface. This is the vertical height of a lower-case letter, such as 'a' (not letters with ascenders or descenders, such as 'h' or 'y').

Grid units of measurement can be based on the pixels (px), which are relative to the screen resolution and only use whole numbers; or percentages (%) which allow for user-control of the size of screen used; or on ems. The em is favoured in CSS3 to lay out grids. An em is relative to the size of a typeface's current point size. It has finer size increments and it scales well.

Understanding the importance of 'white space' (negative space) allows the hierarchy of the design to be revealed and enables the eye to quickly find content and to have moments of rest. The aesthetic skill of a graphic designer can make a design fit to a grid, while keeping the grid invisible. Working against the grid may also be useful if the UI design needs to communicate energy and movement. But working with no grid at all only contributes to poor design decisions.

3.1

optimized size 600 x 300px (browser resolution 640 x 480)

optimized size 760 x 420px (browser resolution 800 x 600)

optimized size 955 x 600px (browser resolution 1024 x 768)

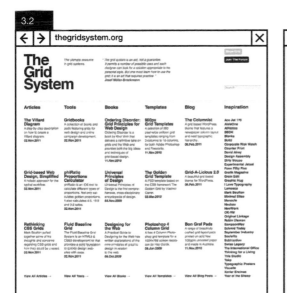

3.2

Considering the screen

The UI elements to be placed in the grid are defined as modules. These are repeatable components defined from image sizes, video player sizes, and so on, on both their x-axis and y-axis. As repeatable rectangular modular components, they are easy to arrange on the gridded screen. However, not all screens are the same.

Design teams working on UIs for TV display need to consider whether the screen will be displayed as a standard (UK/US) 4:3 ratio or as a widescreen (UK/US) 16:9 ratio. The difference in ratios has a direct influence on gridding as the edges of the display on different TVs vary. Any important navigation or content that bleeds off the screen at the edges may be lost if this is not taken into account. To avoid this, designers need to ensure that navigation and content modules are placed within the defined action safe area (inset within the screen) for the chosen screen ratio.

The flexible 12-column grid

A 12-column grid can be reduced to 2-, 3-, 4- or 6-column variations. There are several popular gridded systems in UI design that come from web design: 960px, 976px, or 1140px width grids. Within the 960px width grid, 12 columns would be 60px wide. Each column would have a buffer of 10px each side, allowing for a 20px gutter between columns. In the 1140px grid, 12 columns would be 84px wide with a gutter of 24px. Both have their benefits.

3.3
Mafia II
This screenshot from Take Two's game *Mafia II* has an overlay of action and text safe areas within a screen ratio of 4:3. The outer red rectangle shows the area where action remains visible across all TV screens set at 4:3. The inner yellow rectangle shows where content that is textual will be safe.

3.4
Suggested gridded layout
The BBC GEL (Global Experience Language) guidelines suggest how to set out navigation, content and the styling elements on top of the underlying grid. The grid can be more flexible than these suggestions as other variations are possible (see page 52).

Action Safe Area

Text Safe Area

$1,086.45

The Body Shop

REPAINT $104.00

Change the color to legalize your car

LEAVE ◁▷ BROWSE SHOP BROWSE COLORS

3.3

BBC Sign in   News Sport Weather iPlayer TV Radio More ▾ Search
BACKGROUND TOP & BOTTOM

BBC Sign in   News Sport Weather iPlayer TV Radio More ▾ Search
BACKGROUND LEFT & RIGHT

BBC Sign in   News Sport Weather iPlayer TV Radio More ▾ Search
CONTAINED BANNER

BBC Sign in   News Sport Weather iPlayer TV Radio More ▾ Search
FULL BACKGROUND IMAGE

3.4

Gridding: bespoke or dynamically fluid?

Tablets and smartphones provide an interesting dilemma for the UI designer. A screen can flip from portrait to landscape orientation in response to a simple hand rotation, and the UI has to instantly rearrange all the layout, navigation and content to match the view. An iPad has a screen ratio of 4:3 whilst an Android tablet has a ratio just over 16:9, so any app or website needs to be designed with these variations in mind.

This puts a strain on effective designs, as the underlying grid needs to structure the page in two orientations at once. These problems are being solved through the intersection of clever coding and clear layout, achieved through collaboration between the graphic designer and developer.

The design team will either design the UI to fit each platform (web, tablet, OS etc) separately; or use jQuery code to define which platform is being used. The UI can then determine the screen size available and make itself fluid, resizing its layout to fit. Responsive design is just such a method used in web design. Using CSS3 media queries to determine the device and the size of the display, the code resizes the layout and content to suit the device.

The difference between the display of a website on a desktop and a tablet will be small, but significant. Likewise, the display of an app's UI on a smartphone and on a tablet will be very similar. In each case, a responsively designed fluid grid will optimize the UI through jQuery code to display in the best format for the device.

3.5
Dynamic grid ratios
On the left is a layout on an iPad in 4:3 ratio, and on the right an Android tablet with a ratio of 16:9. It is clear how the fluid gridding of the layout doesn't just translate between ratios and orientation views. The typography and image size are in conflict (as can be seen by the overflowing image in the top right image). The layout needs to be set in the code relative to the orientation and each device's constraints.

3.6
Dynamic grids
The underlying code needs to optimize the layout responsively for each screen ratio and viewing style. The scaling of the text and image is critical to creating responsive designs for each platform and helps avoid distortion when flipping between orientations (left-hand side images are portrait views – right-hand side images are landscape).

3.5

 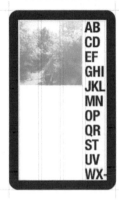

4:3

16:9

3.6

Functionally and aesthetically, typography allows written content to flow and differentiate itself from other content within the UI. The thoughtful selection of the most suitable typeface, at the correct size for the reader, aids the communication of meaning. To achieve this communication, typography manipulates typefaces through word height, letter style and spacing between words, letters and lines. As such, typography gives the designer control over the readability, tone and form of the UI's text, but this must work with the underlying grid in order to be effective.

Typeface classifications

Display
a typeface that is suited to short headlines and notices (Impact)

Monospaced
each letter's width is exactly the same (Courier)

Sans serif
a sans serif is a letter without a serif (Helvetica)

Serif
a serif is a bar that sticks out from each letter's top and/or bottom (Times)

Typefaces or fonts: typography 101

The textual content and navigation of a UI is made intelligible, readable and findable through the selection and manipulation of each typeface. Typefaces can be manipulated in three ways: kerning, tracking and leading. By adjusting these elements, the graphic designer can optimize both the aesthetics and functionality of the written content.

Kerning

Kerning allows the movement of one letter nearer to or farther from its closest neighbour. This adjustment focuses on the negative spaces that words create and maximizes the balance and rhythm of the letters to facilitate scanning and comprehension.

Tracking

Tracking allows the horizontal spaces between words to be increased or decreased. The optimal number of words per line is 12 to 15. Too much tracking between words will reduce readability. Too little, and the effect will be the same.

Leading

Leading allows an increase or decrease in spacing between baselines, and can have dramatic effects on readability. Vertical spacing that is too tight can cause text to look cramped. Too much spacing can also adversely affect readability.

3.7

Cap height
x height
Baseline
Descender line

Em

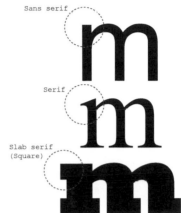

Sans serif

Serif

Slab serif
(Square)

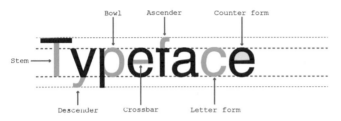

Bowl   Ascender   Counter form

Stem →

Descender   Crossbar   Letter form

Negative
Kerning   Kerning

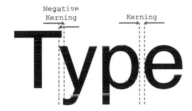

Collisions
happen if
the leading
is too tight

Allow for the
descenders
when setting
leading depth

3.7
Anatomy of a typeface
As can be seen in these
diagrams, the anatomy
of a typeface is complex.
Structurally, the typeface can
ascend up to the Cap Height
above the size of a lower-case
letter (x-height), or below the
baseline to the descender line
for those letters such as
lower-case y and g.
Typography manipulates the
typeface through leading,
tracking and kerning to ensure
reading clarity, and also to
create personality in the text.

Typography for UIs

The complete control a graphic designer has over static type in print is not the same with UI design, as user-control makes UI typography more dynamic. With touchscreen smartphones and tablets, the input is now far more direct than on a PC with a mouse. As such, the leading on a tablet device needs to accommodate input via a fingertip; and on a smartphone, some input is made using the thumb. Since a thumb is broader than a fingertip, the leading needs to be sufficient to allow this kind of input as well.

Therefore, for the same UI to appear on a desktop, a tablet and a smartphone, variations of the UI will need to be available. This can be achieved either by designing and coding responsively, or making different versions for each platform to accommodate the necessary typographic variations.

A UI on a smartphone, as opposed to a PC, is likely to have fewer available links, increased leading and reduced type size. With web UIs some typographic advances in formatting coding have balanced out the user-control, allowing the typography to work more dynamically. In designing web UIs, CSS3 has given the designer more control than ever before over how type is displayed.

Calls to action and visual affordances

Within a UI, the areas of the interface that are interactive, and therefore clickable, need to be clear to the user. HTML-coded websites have a standard where blue underlined text indicates a link. Other interactive elements usually indicate their 'clickability' when the cursor pointer changes to a finger. These are referred to as 'visual affordances' – they communicate a call to action that will lead to an outcome.

3.8

Leading needs
to comfortably
fit the fingertip.

3.8
Type for fingertips
On a smartphone or tablet,
the amount of space for call to
actions needs to be operated by
a fingertip. Leading that is too
tight will result in an overlap of
each link's active areas, which
would cause confusion.

Type on screen

Not all typefaces are optimized for screen use. Those that the Web inherited from print, such as Times and Helvetica, were not designed with pixels in mind. But typefaces such as Georgia and Verdana were designed for pixel display. A reader's tolerance to reading and understanding text on a screen is variable. People read around 10 per cent more slowly on a screen than with printed matter, and in reality scan more than they actually read in full.

Text in a UI can take different forms: navigation, calls to action, captions, headings and blocks of textual content (body copy). The body copy needs to sit in the UI within a hierarchical context (so the reader knows what is most important and the order in which content should be read). This content needs to be clearly defined next to navigational elements, image and video content, so the use of columns to break up the text is crucial. This is why the relationship between typography and the layout's underlying grid is symbiotic.

Serif typefaces are fine as headers, but sans serif typefaces are safer for body copy as they work consistently at any scale. Serif typefaces in body copy at small sizes make the text harder to read. Display, decorative script or black letter typefaces should never be used for body copy, navigation or captions, as readability is compromised.

It is advisable, to avoid setting blocks of text in a grid column as justified (straight left/right edges), centred (except captions) or in capitals (often seen as shouting). Body copy should be legible and easy to 'scan-read'. To help the legibility of body copy, it is good to set paragraphs of text within a grid column flush left. If each paragraph has either a 1em indent at the beginning, or a line between paragraphs, it helps the user to scan the text.

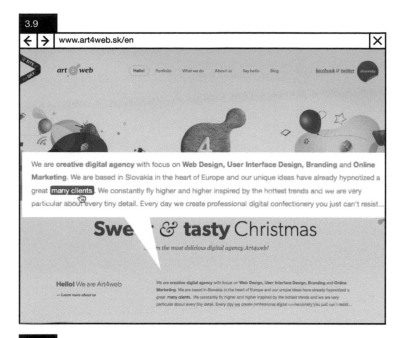

3.9

3.10

Header 36px

Subheader 20px

TIME STAMPS 11Px CAPITALS

Copy 13px Arial Bold on 16px leading Lorem ipsum dolor sit amet, consectetur adipiscing elit. Fusce sed leo. Maecenas ultrices lorem sit amet diam. Aliquam sollicitudin tristique nulla.

Copy 13px Arial Regular on 16px leading Lorem ipsum dolor sit amet, consectetur adipiscing elit. Fusce sed leo. Maecenas ultrices lorem sit amet diam. Aliquam sollicitudin tristique nulla.

▷ **Link Suspendisse porta commodo leo. 13px**

◀)) **Link Pellentesque mollis nisi eget purus 13px**

▢ **COMMENTS 11PX CAPITAL**
✉ **EMAIL 11PX CAPITAL**
🖶 **PRINT 11PX CAPITAL**

⊥ 8px

3.9
Type as interface
Within the written content of the UI, the copy can itself become the interface. Web design was built upon hypertext links moving from page to page via words turned into navigation. The blue underlined link is a basic visual affordance that the word is a link to a call to action – although the coloured text shown here is also a clear call to action.

3.10
Type hierarchy in grids
In implementing a visual hierarchy in a grid with type, the baseline becomes important. In this example, various type-based interface elements range in text height sizes from 36px down to 11px, and are given various different weights (bold, capitals, normal). But each line of text is aligned to a baseline with the leading suitably adjusted to ensure that it remains readable.

Graphic design for print and screen use two different colour space models. Print uses a CMYK colour space of four colours: cyan, magenta, yellow and black, whereas screens use an RGB colour space of red, green and blue. The RGB colour model is referred to as an 'additive model' as it adds together the red, green and blue to create all the visible colours. Beyond the technical and mathematical structures of colour lies its effect. Colour is effective in non-verbal communication as it affects our emotions on a subconscious level. From a hierarchical perspective, colour attracts and guides the eye around an interface. It is useful for separating and distinguishing blocks of content from one another, critically identifying single objects and contrasting relationships between groups of objects.

Displaying colours

Modern screens can display 65,000 colours per pixel, depending upon resolution and the graphics card of the device. However, not every monitor or device is calibrated in the same way, so there are still traditionally only 216 colours that are deemed 'web-safe'. Colour on web-based UIs is controlled by the code through a conversion of the RGB values into a hexadecimal value. The values that make up the range of hexadecimal colours begins at 0 and goes up to 9, and use the letters A to F. Hexadecimally, white (RGB value of 0) reads as the code #FFFFFF, and black (RGB value of 255) as #000000, with every other colour registering values between these extremes (see page 84).

Hexadecimal colour values are used in the Web UI's structure in the HTML, or in the UI's styling within the CSS3 code. With the addition of an alpha channel for creating transparencies, the web designer can create graphically rich designs without the need for too many images. In other UIs, such as apps, BD/DVDs and game interfaces, the RGB colour values are selected either in the UI authoring software or directly referenced in the programming language by the developer.

3.11
Screen-based colours
Screen-based colours are displayed here in both their coded values. The six-digit hexadecimal value of the colour and the corresponding RGB and HSV values are listed next to each colour swatch.

001	031	061	091
ffffff	c02f95	1ca669	c7792a
R 100% G 100% B 100%	R 75.3% G 18.3% B 58.3%	R 10.8% G 65.1% B 41.1%	R 78.0% G 47.4% B 16.5%
002	032	062	092
fff9a8	943e97	6fc1aa	ca9202
R 100% G 97.8% B 65.9%	R 58% G 24.4% B 59.2%	R 43.6% G 75.7% B 65.6%	R 79.2% G 57.2% B 0.9%
003	033	063	093
fefcd3	5b3391	b9d996	fbd200
R 99.6% G 98.8% B 82.8%	R 35.9% G 20.1% B 56.9%	R 72.7% G 85.1% B 58.7%	R 98.4% G 82.3% B 0%
004	034	064	094
f2eb00	6053a3	80c474	ecb500
R 94.9% G 92% B 0%	R 37.6% G 32.6% B 63.9%	R 50.1% G 79.5% B 45.5%	R 92.5% G 71.2% B 0%
005	035	065	095
ebe943	5b3a95	52b447	ae7f2d
R 92.2% G 91.2% B 26.4%	R 35.6% G 22.7% B 58.4%	R 32% G 70.6% B 28%	R 68.2% G 50.1% B 17.7%
000	036	066	096
ffef00	325c97	2ca33f	8b712d
R 100% G 93.6% B 0%	R 19.5% G 23.7% B 59.2%	R 17.3% G 63.9% B 24.6%	R 54.5% G 44.2% B 17.7%
007	037	067	097
fff22f	2a368c	41732a	784800
R 100% G 88.6% B 0%	R 16.6% G 21.8% B 54.9%	R 25.4% G 45.1% B 16.4%	R 47.1% G 28.3% B 0%
008	038	068	098
ffe200	2b479f	064822	764602
R 100% G 94.9% B 18.4%	R 16.9% G 27.8% B 62.4%	R 2.3% G 28.2% B 13.3%	R 46.3% G 27.4% B 0.7%
009	039	069	099
fcdb00	003a5a	184d21	784804
R 98.8% G 85.9% B 0%	R 0% G 38.0% B 53.3%	R 9.4% G 30.2% B 13%	R 47.1% G 28.2% B 1.7%
010	040	070	100
f8c701	024786	195a22	492600
R 97.3% G 78.1% B 0.4%	R 0.6% G 27.9% B 52.5%	R 9.4% G 35.3% B 13.4%	R 28.6% G 14.8% B 0%
011	041	071	101
f8be0e	007ac3	5d6c2b	a4630e
R 97.3% G 74.5% B 5.3%	R 0% G 47.7% B 76.5%	R 36.3% G 42.4% B 16.9%	R 64.3% G 38.9% B 5.5%
012	042	072	102
f4a320	2072bc	d0b101	5ele02
R 95.7% G 63.9% B 12.4%	R 12.4% G 44.9% B 73.7%	R 81.6% G 69.4% B 0.3%	R 36.9% G 11.6% B 0.7%
013	043	073	103
e97705	0163ac	a3bf18	210e00
R 91.4% G 46.7% B 1.8%	R 0.3% G 38.6% B 67.5%	R 63.8% G 74.8% B 9.4%	R 13.9% G 5.4% B 0%
014	044	074	104
e65811	75ace2	7a972b	45413e
R 90.2% G 34.6% B 6.7%	R 45.9% G 67.6% B 88.6%	R 47.6% G 59.2% B 17%	R 27.1% G 12.5% B 24.3%
015	045	075	105
d93f27	a8d1f1	627838	67645d
R 85.1% G 24.7% B 15.4%	R 66% G 81.9% B 94.5%	R 38.1% G 47.1% B 22%	R 40.4% G 39.2% B 36.4%
016	046	076	106
e5493a	0074bf	87a991	89867f
R 89.8% G 28.5% B 22.9%	R 0% G 45.3% B 74.9%	R 52.9% G 66.3% B 56.9%	R 53.7% G 52.5% B 49.8%
017	047	077	107
e21920	029be0	853a32	a5a29b
R 88.6% G 9.7% B 12.4%	R 0.7% G 60.9% B 87.9%	R 52.2% G 22.9% B 19.6%	R 64.7% G 63.6% B 60.9%
018	048	078	108
e33841	029be0	581f05	c5c2bb
R 89.1% G 22.1% B 25.4%	R 0.7% G 40.9% B 87.8%	R 34.5% G 12.3% B 1.9%	R 77.3% G 76.1% B 73.3%
019	049	079	109
e2172h	24b0ea	bc0347	dcd5cf
R 88.6% G 9% B 17%	R 14% G 69% B 91.8%	R 73.7% G 1.2% B 27.8%	R 86.3% G 83.6% B 81.2%
020	050	080	110
a92713	0078aa	9f0158	e4e3e8
R 66.3% G 15.4% B 7.2%	R 0% G 47.2% B 66.7%	R 62.4% G 0.5% B 34.6%	R 89.5% G 89.2% B 91%
021	051	081	111
b32937	0071b0	b87cb2	cacaca
R 70.2% G 16% B 21.4%	R 0% G 44.7% B 69.6%	R 72.2% G 48.7% B 69.6%	R 79.2% G 79.2% B 79.2%
022	052	082	112
cc2e46	008191	ec8e8f	a8afb5
R 80% G 18.2% B 27.5%	R 0% G 50.7% B 56.9%	R 92.3% G 55.5% B 56.1%	R 68% G 68.7% B 71%
023	053	083	113
d5064b	0092b1	ef987e	78777c
R 83.3% G 2.3% B 29.4%	R 0% G 57.2% B 69.4%	R 93.7% G 59.7% B 49.3%	R 47.1% G 46.7% B 48.6%
024	054	084	114
e1075e	92d4e0	f4c2b9	78777c
R 88.2% G 2.6% B 37.1%	R 57.3% G 83% B 87.8%	R 95.7% G 75.9% B 72.4%	R 47.1% G 46.7% B 48.6%
025	055	085	115
e96175	00a3b4	da9776	162e38
R 91.4% G 38% B 46%	R 0% G 64.1% B 70.6%	R 85.3% G 59.4% B 46.3%	R 8.6% G 18.1% B 22%
026	056	086	116
e34f9c	006b65	cc6952	01011b
R 89% G 31.1% B 61.1%	R 0% G 42% B 39.5%	R 80% G 41.1% B 32.3%	R 0.4% G 0.4% B 10.6%
027	057	087	117
e3008c	17c5e	9a5546	02000d
R 89% G 0% B 55%	R 0.4% G 46.6% B 36.9%	R 60.4% G 33.5% B 27.5%	R 0.6% G 0% B 5.1%
028	058	088	118
ab1a54	019064	b86843	b2b2b2
R 67.1% G 10.3% B 33%	R 0.4% G 56.5% B 39.1%	R 72.2% G 40.6% B 26.3%	R 69.8% G 69.8% B 69.8%
029	059	089	119
d080b6	01ae9b	d67c2d	c0a86c
R 81.6% G 50.2% B 71.2%	R 0.3% G 68.2% B 60.8%	R 83.9% G 48.7% B 17.8%	R 75.3% G 65.9% B 42.2%
030	060	090	120
f3b7d3	000683	ab700a	916c4f
R 95.3% G 71.6% B 82.9%	R 0% G 2.6% B 51.5%	R 67% G 43.9% B 3.9%	R 56.9% G 42.2% B 31%

The meanings of colour

On a basic level, colour affects our perceptions. It can help determine how a user will perceive the UI design, its navigation and its content. But beware, colour is psychologically and culturally defined, having different meanings within different cultures around the world.

People generally perceive warm colours as brighter and more dominant. Warm colours pull forward, expanding and popping out from their backgrounds. Cold colours do the opposite and rush backward. Neutral colours have less impact, emotionally and perceptively. Colour is excellent at defining a visual experience, stimulating liveliness and interest or calming the viewer.

In most western countries, people with different languages can still share the same interpretation of colour – for example, red can represent danger or passion. But some colours can prove problematic as their meanings within different cultures can be diverse. Green, for instance, is associated with ecology and nature in the West. But in non-western cultures, it can also mean corruption and infidelity. So although colour is useful in UI design for conveying personality, tone, information and calls to action, it should be used in conjunction with image and text to maximize communication and minimize potential misunderstandings.

3.12a

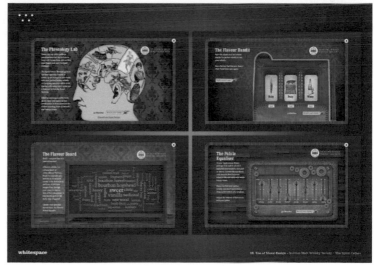

3.12a–3.12b
Colour perception changes
The selection of a suitable colour palette will help convey the correct tone and message to the user. In these examples the Scotch Malt Whisky Society uses a muted and earthy palette of colours to hint at a secret buried deep down underground. The Edinburgh Fringe website uses a more vibrant palette of warmer colours to suggest the creativity during the month-long cultural festival.

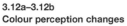

Applying colour

Colours are always relative to the context in which they are viewed. By grouping two or three colours together into a scheme, combinations can be found that work well for the UI design. A colour wheel can be used when choosing colours for screen (RGB) or print (CMYK). A colour wheel comprises a spectrum based upon the three primary pigment colours of red, blue and yellow.

Complementary colours sit opposite each other on the colour wheel (such as red and green). Analogous colours sit next to each other and work well together as they share a similar part of the spectrum (such as green, blue and purple). By selecting a three-colour scheme, a triadic relationship can be established. The RGB colour space offers the widest range of triadic relationships for selecting and viewing colours.

In triadic relationships, colours need to be balanced to ensure the UI will be usable, as some colour combinations are problematic. Contrast within colours shows levels of importance through prominence. By selecting three colours for a colour scheme, you can go for all complementary or analogous colours. Clashing colours add too much 'noise' to a design and should be avoided, but contrasting colours can be effective to draw attention.

3.13
Colour theory
Colour theory is a foundational part of visual communication. Within this diagram compiled from mudcu.be/sphere/, the relationships between complementary, analogous and neutral colours can be understood.

RGB – additive colour and hexadecimal values

Additive colour

Red, green and blue light is projected with a value between 0 and 255 to provide all the other visible colours. If all the RGB colours are at their lowest intensity of zero (switched off) then white light is projected. If they are all projected at their fullest intensity (all switched on to a value of 255) then black light is projected. In web UI design, these RGB values are converted into markup code: HTML uses hexadecimal values and CSS3 use RGBA values. RGBA also allows for transparency (the 'A' represents the alpha channel that controls the colour's opacity).

Hexadecimal values

Red's own hexadecimal value is #FF0000 (red turned on, green and blue turned off), green's is #00FF00 (green turned on, red and blue turned off), and blue's is #0000FF (blue turned on, red and green turned off).

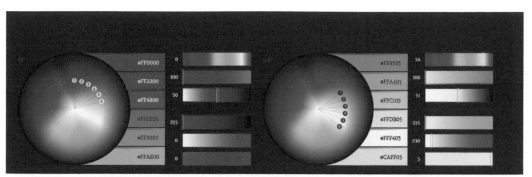

Neutral reds

Neutral yellows

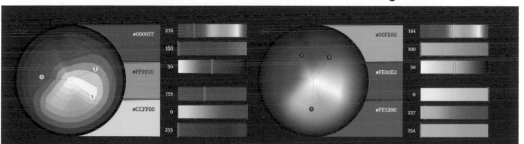

Neutral blues

Clashing colours

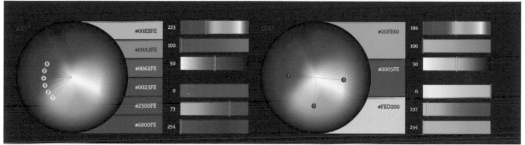

Complementary colours (websafe)

Split complementary colours

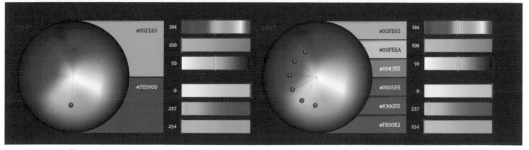

Complementary colours

Analogous colours

3.13

In UI design, images can function as content, decoration and, crucially, as navigation. Understanding how to use images is essential for the designer. Images displayed on computer screens are different to printed images, although they share common requirements of quality, resolution and copyright clearance.

Traditionally, desktop displays have focused on a minimum resolution of 72ppi (pixels per inch). Screen quality of images beyond 72ppi was perceived as being a waste of file size. With modern tablet displays, however, the total resolution has now increased the pixel density up to 326ppi, which is higher than the standard 300ppi minimum required for print.

Images for screen

Digital image files fall into two categories: vectors and bitmaps. Vectors have very small file sizes and are created mathematically, whereas bitmaps are created through colouring each pixel in the image.

The screen is a grid of pixels and an image displays itself within that grid, with each pixel being one of at least 256 colours (at low screen resolutions). This means that a realistic image, such as a photo, keeps its lifelike quality by displaying within this colour range. To achieve this, the bitmap uses anti-aliasing, blurring two coloured pixels with a third pixel that is a mix of the two. This creates the illusion of smoothness, compensating for the stepped nature of pixels.

As a set number of pixels define a bitmap image's quality and integrity, resizing is a problem. When shrinking a bitmap, the image will lose quality because pixels are being removed. For example, if an 800x600px image is reduced to a 400x300px size, there are 360,000 fewer pixels with which to display the same image. Enlarging a bitmap also affects the quality as adding pixels reduces the integrity of the original image.

Vector images, on the other hand, do not lose image integrity in resizing, as the integrity of vectors is mathematically controlled and infinitely scalable without loss of quality. Vector file formats, such as encapsulated postscript files (EPS), are great for printing, but their large file size means they are not suitable for UI design.

Within UI design (predominantly web design) scalable vector graphic (SVG) files are used. SVG is a text-based language (supported in Adobe Illustrator) to draw and animate images for online display. It mathematically describes the shapes, paths, filter effects and type that define the finished image. An SVG image doesn't suffer from any loss of integrity when resized.

3.14

3.15

Image file formats

EPS – Encapsulated PostScript.
Print file format.

GIF – Graphics Interchange Format.
Works well for line-based images, typography
or simple flat colour (no longer widely used).

JPG – Joint Photographic Experts Group.
Works well for continuous-tone photographs
in RGB.

PNG – Portable Network Graphic. Works
well when mixing text and image together.

SVG – Scalable Vector Graphic. Not a file
format, but a text-based language (XML);
SVGs use vector coordinates to define the
dynamic construction of images in a browser.

3.14
Bitmap and vector images
Within this image, the
comparison between icons
created as a bitmap (left) and
icons created as a vector (right)
is clear. When magnified, the
vector image remains sharper
than the bitmap. The bitmap's
edges can clearly be seen as
being pixelated and anti-aliased.

3.15
Anti-aliasing
The anti-aliasing can be
seen by zooming in to see
the bitmapped icon's edge.
The green icon and the grey
background use overlapping
gradations of each colour to
soften the edge. When viewed
at 100 per cent, this tricks the
eye into seeing the edge as
smooth rather than jagged.

Images as navigation

Navigation can be represented in various metaphorical visual forms (tabs, menus, hypertext, buttons, etc). In some UI designs, images can visually integrate all the required interaction into a contextually themed user experience. This then seamlessly makes the image itself into both content and navigation, but care should be taken to ensure that the visual affordances are obvious.

By creating a visual environment for the interface to work through, an image can indicate interaction whilst still maintaining the visual metaphor. To do this the image needs to follow some real-world logic to remain coherent. Within game UIs the UI design normally does this by visually integrating the aesthetics, identity and tone of the game world into the interactive selection process.

One way to understand 'image as navigation' is to consider the UI as a visually represented environment, instead of it being a container of images, text, animation and navigation in an obvious gridded layout.

3.16
Embedded interaction
Within this contextual image, additional navigation takes the form of buttons and icons integrated into the message post image. The interaction is embedded into the image and forms a visual whole, rather than sitting awkwardly on top of the image as a navigation bar.
www.sensisoft.com

Iconography

The benefit of using an image as a visual context is its coherence to the user as a metaphor. But 'image as navigation' will not work for every UI design. It is just one more tool in the designer's conceptual toolbox to be used when it will be beneficial to the user (and client).

Iconography and visual communication have a long heritage, stretching back thousands of years, right back to ancient Egypt and even prehistoric cave paintings. The imagery in this early art contained rich symbolic and metaphorical representations of animals and rituals, which were clearly meaningful to the people who created them. Today, we use symbols and icons in our written and visual language in much the same way: a small image or a line represents a bigger idea.

Since the development of the graphical user interface in the 1970s through the early innovations of graphic designers, such as Norm Cox, Karen Elliott and Susan Kare, the use of icons in UI design has grown and matured. As users, we are now familiar with icon metaphors representing documents, folders, control panels, settings files, drivers and disks.

As humans, we make subconscious connections to the UI interactive functions through the use of such metaphors. The use of icons in a UI makes it easy to differentiate interactive elements from more static content.

3.16

← → www.sensisoft.com ✕

← → www.sensisoft.com ✕

Icons: complex processes made easy

Icons are interface tools that visually focus attention and communicate, in a concise way, a call to action through an understandable visual metaphor. Understanding the connection between the icon and the function leads to a desired action being taken (usually clicking) and a successful outcome.

The icon needs to clearly convey its function to the user. As interpretation of imagery is culturally situated and ambiguous, the image the icon adopts needs to be familiar and instantly recognizable. If it is not, the action will not be communicated.

The image may be specifically connected to the function or be representational or abstract. The more specific the image is, the easier it is to connect to the function and action; if it is obtuse, it will have to be learned by the user.

There is an established iconic vocabulary with a rich and complex grammar of its own that users are familiar with. Meanings are either learned (house = homepage icon) or instantly identifiable (printer = print) by the user.

If the meaning of an envelope has been established as 'email', changing its function will mislead the user. Bad use of icons is down to the designer. Too often, interfaces fail because icons are used in navigation without any sense of meaning.

Established icon vocabulary:

Cog – settings

Envelope – email

House – home page

Magnifying glass – search or enlarge

Printer – print

3.17
Icon sets
Icons need to convey a call to action, so its imagery needs to stand out from the UI's content without competing with it. If these icons were not labelled, how many would be obvious, and how many would need to be learned?

3.17

Information	Upload to cloud	Chat
Link to this	Like	Download
Refresh	Search	Shopping cart

Metaphor and context

Metaphor is a particularly useful tool in visual communication as it can cut through cross-generational or cross-cultural complexities. Essentially, it is the transfer of meaning from one object to another. It is a very common device in written and spoken language.

Metaphors have had a persistent role since the GUI's original desktop metaphors of folders, files etc. A suitable UI metaphor is one that explains the function and facilitates action instantaneously. But it must also be readily understandable, readable and contextually relevant to a large number of users (often across multiple languages).

Adding text labels to icons helps optimize usability, as some iconic meaning will take time to learn. Before the home page icon of a house became universally adopted, it had a text label saying 'home' next to it. Once an icon's identity and purpose becomes universally accepted, it can live on its own in a UI without labelling.

Once a universal meaning has been established, the rich visual language and grammar of icons can become a source of design inspiration. There isn't just one way to draw a house, a magnifying glass or an envelope – designers have found various innovative ways to represent these universal icons.

Icon design software

— AWicons Pro by Lokas Software

— IconWorkshop by Axialis Software

— Icon Craft by Icon Empire

3.18
Meanings of icons
If you covered up the labels of these icons, then different users may interpret each image differently. Visual communication in icons fails when the metaphor or analogy is not clearly understood. If a universal meaning has yet to be established then the addition of textual labels is crucial to aid user understanding.

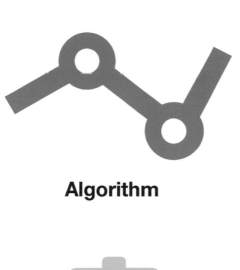

Algorithm

Wiki

Spam Analysis

Optimization

Download

Review

3.18

Designing icon families

Designing an icon is not as simple as making an image and then scaling it down. Icon images – being a representation of a more complex function – require a different approach to images used for content. Due to the utility of an icon, it needs to operate at a variety of scales, at different resolutions and on a variety of screen displays. Although icons are bitmap images, they cannot be anti-aliased in the way that content imagery can be.

The icon must display and communicate at different scales using differing numbers of pixels. The imagery used for an icon needs to appear the same at 512x512px and 32x32px, despite there being a difference of 261,120 pixels between the two sizes.

This imposes severe restraints, which need to be carefully considered. Bitmap images made up of a grid of square pixels work best when they incorporate right angles. At such small sizes, without anti-aliasing to aid smoothing the lines, angles can become very important. A pixel out of line either way can ruin the icon design.

The icon will also need to work at different resolutions of colour display. A 256 colour 8-bit version will be needed, as well as a 16 colour 4-bit version for lower resolution displays. In some cases, a monochrome version may be required, meaning that a 1-bit icon would have to be simplified from the previous colour versions.

The development of icon design has a solid technical and creative basis, and will continue to offer exciting challenges to designers as higher resolution screen displays offer a greater range of colours.

Problems with pixels and angles

45° angles can work, but when the angles change to 30°, 60° or 120° problems can become really noticeable in a grid of square pixels. Any other angles, or circles and ellipses can become really problematic when displayed in a square grid.

3.19
Icon sizes and resolution
An icon needs to be designed carefully and methodically in icon families of multiple sizes to aid legibility. In each icon family there will be at least six to eight pieces of artwork that operate at different scales. Each icon would first be developed through sketching before designing in software.

3.19

Core iPhone and app launcher icon sizes

29 x 29px   50 x 50px   57 x 57px   58 x 58px   72 x 72px   114 x 114px

512 x 512px

With interaction becoming more embodied, motion in interfaces has moved from animations and motion graphics to embedded streaming video players and motion-sensitive inputs. Graphic designers aren't involved in the coding or the innovation of these new technologies, but that doesn't mean they have no role in these changes. Graphic design should be taken into account in the way a video player is embedded into an interface, and how the design of an interface will react to the motion inputs to create an aesthetic user experience.

Interfacing motion as an experience

Whether designing interfaces for websites, software, apps, DVDs or computer games, the use of motion in the UI is changing. Websites used to use third party plug-ins to accommodate playing animations or video – now the code can control this. Software and apps incorporated motion into the UIs to aid the experience – in some cases motion is the primary input.

Innovations in the computer games industry, specifically with Nintendo's Wii and Microsoft's Kinect, are seeding across into other forms of software. With the proliferation of tablet computing, such as the iPad utilizing motion sensors alongside the touch screen and voice control, input is changing from the mouse to the human body. This is making the personal computer even more personal, and the visual communication of the interface must match this.

In some cases, the UI now has to work not only across devices, but also across differing types of input. But the UI still needs to seamlessly deliver the content, the information and a great user experience. Therefore, graphic designers working in UI design need to keep on top of emerging technologies to look for visual solutions in creating motion-based aesthetic user experiences.

3.20
Microsoft's Kinect
Microsoft's Kinect senses the human body and turns it into embodied input, controlling what is seen on the TV screen. Gameplay can now be more physical and media entertainment can be selected without the need for a remote control.

3.20

Visually communicating motion

Apart from showing video and animation, motion is used to communicate content, calls to action or feedback from an interaction. Software-loading sequences incorporate motion, and UI components demonstrate action and processing through motion (for example, loading progress bars). Titles, logos and buttons may have some form of motion attached to them to draw the attention and focus of the user.

Computer games and DVD/BDs use animation to show transitions between changing UI screens and within the interface to draw attention to action calls, or to simply preview parts of the video or game content. Within some interfaces, content selection is animated through the use of slide shows and carousels, enlarging or reducing the image scales to aid selection. An obvious caution to any UI design team (clients take note, too) is to use restraint when using motion to visually communicate.

With the advent of advanced coding (such as HTML5) the need for third-party plug-ins is diminishing, and many opportunities for exciting user experiences can be created – if the designer and developer work collaboratively. Alternative viewing options can also be innovated, such as the UI's background being video-based (this needs to be optimized to prevent a drain on download times). Too much of this just becomes 'noise' that interferes with clear communication, however.

Video content itself is now demanding much more from the design and layout of the UI. The user (also a viewer) needs to feel secure that they still remain in the same interface if they access video (HTML5 does make this easier). So the embedding of media players into web-based or app-based interfaces has implications for effective visual communication.

Websites and apps from TV channel providers (such as the BBC), streaming video providers (such as Netflix), and archived video (such as YouTube) have innovated the look and feel for the new breed of embedded media players. Video content (embedded or streaming) can now be set in the main interface screen, or it can be popped out into its own player window. It can even take over the entire display screen. Therefore, the visual communication of the branding, tone and identity needs to be maintained across all three viewing options.

3.22

3.21
Sick City Club
With Flash-based interfaces, video can directly be embedded as a backdrop to the interface. In the case of a band's website, this makes sense as it helps to reinforce the band's brand with their music at the same time. In other cases, this will probably not work for the user (for example, an insurance UI that plays a video of a salesman discussing insurance policies in the background of the normal UI content).
www.sickcityclub.net

3.22
Coded animation
Motion in UI doesn't just mean media players and video content. Motion can also be coded and controlled by the input (mouse, finger, body). In this example, by shifting the position of the cursor, the camera viewfinder moves around the scene. This is all controlled by underlying code.
http://attackemart.in/camera-parallax-effect/

Role
Graphic web designer, UK

Experience
Professional graphic designer for 14 years

Web
http://mikekus. com/

Some people advise designing a UI from the mobile platform out to the desktop platform. Do you agree?

I think these sorts of sweeping statements are a mistake. It can help, definitely, but I wouldn't say that is the way you have to do it. With all the mobile devices around now, responsive design has come into its own. If you are going to design a website properly – whether you design a responsive site or not – you definitely need to have some sort of mobile solution. Things like the iPad can deal with normal websites quite easily, but for phones it's a whole different thing and you really do need to have some sort of solution for that.

The principles that you use as a graphic designer in print translate pretty much directly across to the Web. All you're doing with the Web as opposed to print is making it fluid – reconfiguring it into a different type of grid as the window size decreases.

Can you give an example of how graphic design principles have translated from print to the Web?

When I first started doing web design it was still just Helvetica, Verdana and Times New Roman, and they were your web fonts. You couldn't really do that much with them.

Not very long afterward TypeKit came out, along with @font-face, and various other web font solutions. They're great – you've got a much bigger range of fonts that render really well on screen, and they'll also work perfectly on an iPhone. So it's amazing what you can do now that it's been brought into line with traditional graphic design.

Can you give an example of how you now apply your visual communication training to web design?

You now get much more complex sites than before, it makes you think about the way you design a website completely from the very beginning. I guess what really changed was the introduction of CSS3 media queries. It changed the styles, and obviously once you're jumping from a three-column grid, to a two-column grid, to a one-column grid you are not only changing the percentages of the columns but what fits into them. You're thinking about how this is going to translate down to a mobile device. You might decide, for example, to increase the weight of the typeface and reduce the point size you are using if you carry on using it on a smaller device. Bear in mind that if you're going to be on a tablet the text doesn't have to be so big – the titles can come down. There are lots of considerations.

3.23

3.23
Future Insights Live
When asked to redesign the
new Future Insights event
websites for 2013 Mike Kus
and Neil Kinnish (who worked
on the front-end development)
created a fully responsive
site, which can be found at:
futureinsightslive.com/
las-vegas-2013/.

Project
Neil Young
Archives, Vol. 1
(1963–1972)
Blu-ray DVD

Design team
Total Media
Group, California,
USA

Client
Shakey Pictures

Planning the Blu-ray UI

Canadian singer-songwriter Neil Young's prolific career has spanned over five decades. He had a vision of releasing an archive of his music and associated memorabilia as an immersive multimedia experience. Blu-ray (BD) technology made this possible.

The design team at Total Media had their work cut out to create a high quality experience to match Neil's expected high-resolution sound quality. He wanted the listener to be able to browse the memorabilia – press, ticket stubs, articles, and photos – directly related to each song as they listen to it.

Neil Young and members of his production company, Shakey Pictures, worked closely with Total Media's Creative Director Toshi Onuki to discuss the look and feel of the experience. A realistic virtual environment was required for the immersion, which also needed to be easily navigated.

Information architecture, gridding and metaphor

Across the archive's ten BD box set there were 3000 menu screens and more than 20 terabytes of material to make into content assets. As Toshi recalls, 'I don't think we really knew how big the project was until we had everything delivered to us'. Every screen on the BDs was a bespoke scenario, and each song was a snapshot of a time featuring contextual memorabilia that could be visually explored by the user. Therefore, every screen also had a bespoke grid.

To manage such a large UI design project, worked on by many different team members, Toshi created a structure to establish clear team communication of the standards and file management protocols that would be needed. Using a metaphor of a 50-year-old display case of document folders, each folder would represent one song, and contain the memorabilia associated with it.

3.24

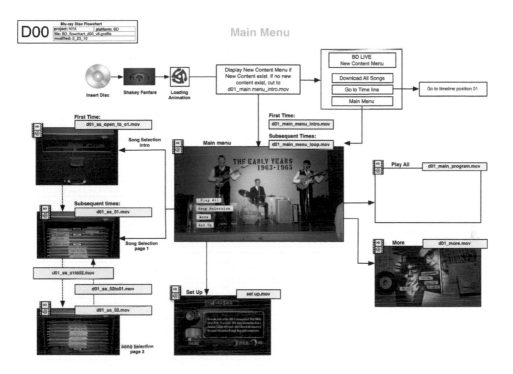

D00	Blu-ray Disc Flowchart
	project: NYA
	platform: BD
	file: BD_flowchart_d00_v6.graffle
	modified: 2_23_10

Main Menu

Insert Disc → Shakey Fanfare → Loading Animation → Display New Content Menu if New Content exist. If no new content exist, cut to d01_main_menu_intro.mov

BD LIVE
New Content Menu
Download All Songs
Go to Time line → Go to timeline position 01
Main Menu

First Time:
d01_ss_open_to_o1.mov

Song Selection intro

First Time:
d01_main_menu_intro.mov

Subsequent Times:
d01_main_menu_loop.mov

Main menu

THE EARLY YEARS
1963-1965

Play All
Song Selection
More
Set Up

Play All — d01_main_program.mov

Subsequent times:
d01_ss_01.mov

Song Selection page 1

More — d01_more.mov

d01_ss_v1to02.mov

d01_ss_02to01.mov

Set Up — set up.mov

d01_ss_02.mov

Song Selection page 2

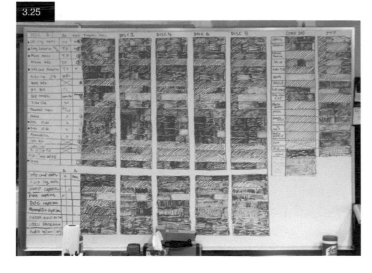

3.24
BD menu
As can be seen from this visual, the BD menu is quite complex. However, the visual metaphor and gridded layout visually communicate what can be selected. In the metaphor of the file drawer, song files are accessible by clicking on the tabs.

3.25
The planning stage
Alongside complex information architecture, a filing system was structured of categories, such as memorabilia, press, photos, etc. Each category in turn had contextual assets, such as thumbnails, photo galleries and captions and sub-screens.

3.25

Icons and motion

As each screen presented a separate
scenario from Neil Young's career,
each navigational icon was also
different and contextual to each
scenario. But each link had to be
obvious to the user, so every link
used a consistent five-frame animation
in its selected state, growing in size
and brightness. This aided exploration
of the UI, answering Neil's desire
for an obsessive immersive
experience. But this required a lot
of design. Each button, in a layered
PSD file, consisted of its normal state,
the selected state and its active state.
With 3000 screens multiplied
by multiple buttons per screen,
this meant a lot of work, which
was only made possible by solid
information architecture.

3.26a – 3.26b
Navigation and
menu selection
Deeper into the DVD content
hierarchy, the richness of
content access is represented
in this diagram overlaid on a
UI screen. The relationships
are highlighted so that when
individually clicked they access
the sub-screens shown in 3.26b.

'Graphically, the Archives
project reflects Neil's
sensibilities very well.
Toshi has a perspective
that only someone
who wasn't in America
during the 60s and 70s
can have. Because he
wasn't prejudiced by
the time period or its
iconic graphics, he could
stand back and look at
the individual images
in the archive for what
they were, and envision
the entire project as an
artistic whole.'
– L. A. Johnson,
Shakey Pictures producer

3.26a

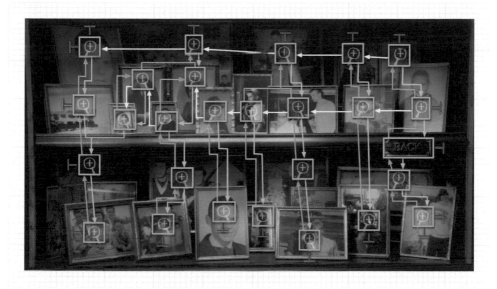

3.26b

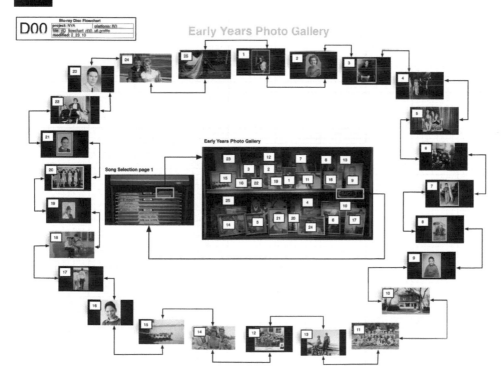

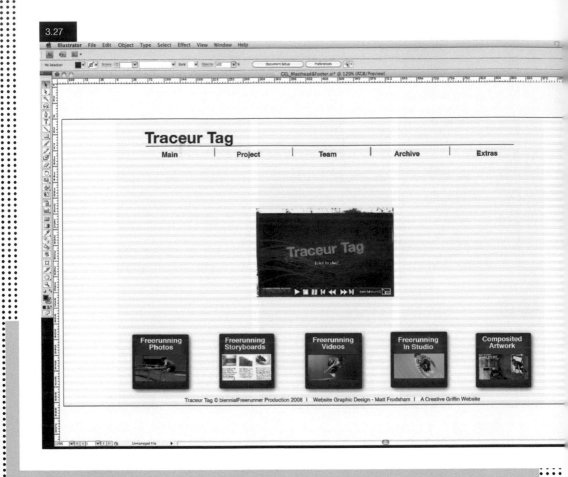

3.27

**3.27
Set the navigation and assets**
Using the grid and the baseline, position the navigation and logo in a new layer called Navigation. Add the other content assets, such as images, icons, footers and even embedded media players into another new layer called Assets. Align these horizontally within the grid's columns and vertically on each baseline.

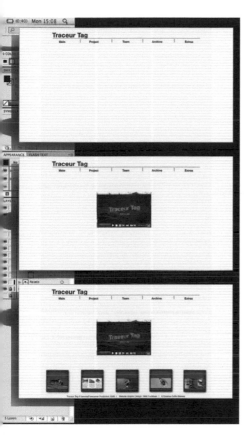

Premise

In this chapter, the key foundations of graphic design for digital media have been discussed. By applying these through visual experimentation, you will become more confident in designing a UI.

This exercise is about visual communication, so the outcome will not be interactive. It can be repeated many times, and adapted as your confidence grows. By selecting the screen resolution, using a grid, applying typographical variations, selecting suitable colours and imagery you can experiment with how best to visually communicate visual affordances and calls to action.

The following resources will be needed:

— Software of choice

   (Adobe Creative Suite is standard. For the purpose of this exercise use whichever software you're currently familiar with).

— A grid – see http://tinyurl.com/examplegrid

— Assets: images, icons, written copy.

(You can use dummy content or content from a previous website you may have designed).

3.28
Set the text to
the baseline
The text forming the body copy of the content is set at 14pxs high, and the leading height is 16pxs. Other text such as the quote, footer, navigation and header have different leading heights in proportion to each different letter height.

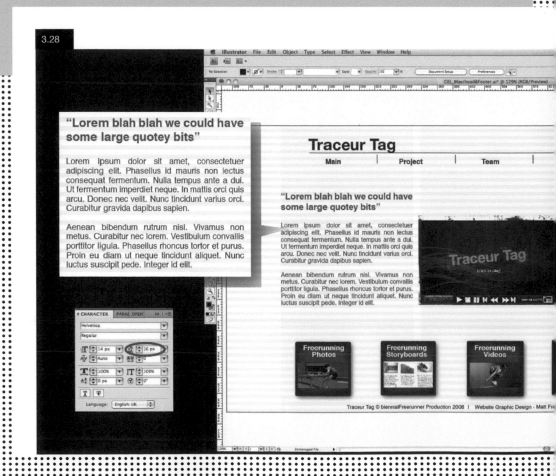

3.28

Exercise

Open the sample 976px desktop grid in your software of choice.

Set the navigation and assets
(see Image 3.27)

Add a new layer called Navigation. Place your navigation on the grid in this layer and align it to an appropriate baseline.

Add the next new layer, called Assets. In this layer, you will place any images or media, aligned appropriately to the grid's columns and baselines. Remember to allow for white (negative) space and don't forget to build a visual hierarchy.

Set the text to the baseline
(see Image 3.28)

Add the last layer, called Text. Add text boxes, with your written copy. Take into account the way in which x-height and baseline heights are linked mathematically together, be prudent in the typefaces you choose.

Once you're happy you have achieved an effective design, hide the Grid layer. You'll now see how the visual communication of the UI works. Toggle the Grid layer on and off to see how the alignment to the grid is working.

Outcomes

You should see a very rough hierarchy of interactions on the wall across the three content levels. Is the revealed interactive structure far more complex than you initially thought it would be? This technique works for any form of UI (DVD/BD, app, even game UI). It makes you deconstruct the complex flow of how content is made accessible to the user.

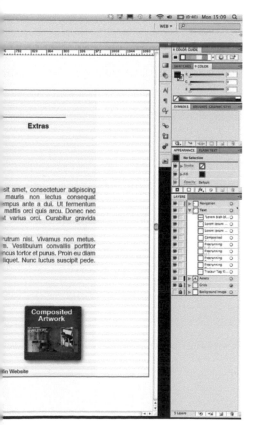

Designing the aesthetic user experience

This chapter explores the specifics of design objectives for user interaction, through tailoring the UI's content to meet the user's objectives and expectations. The aesthetic experience of the person using a UI will be explained through theories relating to the context of use.

As designers are not end users, it is crucial to see each visual affordance to a call of action from the user's point of view; we will therefore examine user interaction from a first-person perspective. We will then explore semiotic theory to illustrate how design for a first-person perspective works.

The user has been championed throughout this book. As has been shown, their presence in the UI design process is central to effective design. But what is this presence? This section will look a little more deeply into the psychology of a user's interaction to help you design an aesthetic experience for them. The user's first-person perspective of interaction is of key importance to the design of a successful aesthetic user experience.

Dynamics of interaction

Although (able-bodied) people interact with the world through the same senses – sight, hearing, smell, touch and taste – not everyone interprets their experiences in the same way. An individual's interpretation is personal, emotional, cognitive and embodied interaction. An aesthetic user experience is one where the user's concern for their own self is temporarily lost in an effortless involvement in the moment, and their sense of time within the interaction is altered.

Interaction can be accidental *('oops, what did I click then?')*, non-intentional *('I'm bored, I'll just browse')*, purposeful *('I definitely want to find this')* as well as goal-orientated *('I expect to achieve this outcome if I click here').* It requires active engagement from the user based upon their emotional and cognitive responses. Therefore, an interface's user experience (UX) is designed to provide agency to the UI's visually communicated calls to action in order to access content.

It is important to remember that designers (and developers) know too much about designing interfaces to appreciate how the novice user views an interface. In large design teams, the UX designer has the responsibility of understanding users' objectives, their context of use and their levels of experience.

Perception is not a passive thing – it is connected to action. Understanding how users perceive and interpret calls to action will allow you to set targeted design objectives for the UI. These objectives will help you to understand what the visual communication outcomes of the UI need to be. In turn, this knowledge will help you to design the UI in such a way that the user will perceive which parts of the UI are interactive.

4.1
Embodied in the world
As we are embodied in the real
world, our own perceptions
of, and the way we interpret,
what we see, hear, taste, smell
and touch help us shape our
individual world. Each person
will perceive and interpret their
interactions in their own way,
but within an interface these
perceptions should be managed
to provide a similar experience
to all users. Image from *The
Catalogue*, a video created by
artist Chris Oakley in 2004.

The first-person experience

A UI will look the same to every user. It will have a designed layout combining content (images, media and written copy) and calls to action (navigation and icons), which allow access to that content. But not every user will have the same prior knowledge or the same aesthetic user experience. For a designer to understand how users will perceive and interpret the interactive experience, it is useful to imagine the interaction through a first-person perspective.

Let's simplify this issue with an analogy. Think of a door as an interface between the internal and external. We all know through past experience that to get from one position to the other (the goal) we need to open the door (the interface) by using a door handle (call to action). But not all doors behave the same way (past experience). Some doors open outwards, some inwards, some rotate and some slide (functionality). Added to this, not all door handles are the same (design). The act of getting from one location to another (the goal) now seems more complicated. But we perceive the type of door, its potential interactions and quickly decide on an action to obtain our goal.

Of course, we've all had the experience of trying to push open a 'pull' door. This is usually because we assume the door will work in the way we've experienced in the past (or we may simply not be paying attention). Users approach digital interfaces in the same way. When interfaces (and doors) fail the individual, it comes down to two factors: expectations and the communication of visual affordances. If a door is to be pushed open, but the handle is a vertical bar which suggests *pull*, people will pull it. We've all done it.

This happens all too often in UI design. Confusing design decisions confound the user's expectations. Designers must understand and appreciate what will communicate a successful visual affordance. Semiotics helps in this (more on this on pages 118–119), but understanding and appreciating a user's first-person perspective, by conducting user research and testing, is invaluable. This perspective will inform your visual communication decisions, ensuring that the UI is communicating the calls to action correctly, making an aesthetic experience achievable.

4.2

4.2
L.A. Noire
In this game UI from L.A. Noire, it is clear that the navigation (1) is the most obvious interactive part. The typography (2) used on the wall is really the main navigation. The use of a chunky typeface (set in uppercase) and the labels ensure the user can perceive these links. Additional navigation is set further back in the scene and may be missed (3).

4.3
IDEO's method cards
Tools, such as IDEO's Method Cards, help the design team frame their ideas to be more in tune with how users will perceive and interpret the interaction. The cards are classified as four suits: 'ask', 'watch', 'learn' and 'try'. www.ideo.com/work/method-cards/.

4.3

Typography is meaningless without words, and UIs without words are not as effective. Written copy in the form of body text, image captions, navigation labels and headings, is important to a successful interface. Therefore, well-written copy, displayed through effective typography, helps create an aesthetic user experience. The quality and conciseness of written copy helps to set an appropriate tone of voice, reflecting the depth of understanding of the target audience. It also helps to clearly facilitate the UI's call to actions, helping the user to identify what needs to be done and in what order.

4.4
Grip Limited
In this website, the combination of typeface, labels, colour and concise copy is effective. The accessible, 'straight talking' copy works well with the clear layout, a good typographical leading ratio, and colour contrast.

The copy reads:

'At Grip Limited we hate the word 'Silo'. We have no preconceived ideas about the form our ideas should take, where they should be placed or how big or small a budget ought to be. Anything goes. It's a clean slate every time. The only constant? Senior people coming up with the best ideas to move out clients' business forward. Whatever the medium, whatever the discipline, whatever the idea.'

Accessibility through good copy

Good content should engage and retain the interest of the UI's users. Too often, copy in a UI is either too lengthy or corporate for its target audience. Since people tend to scan text on a screen display rather than reading it in full, many UIs have far more copy than is actually needed.

All content, especially written content, should have a clear purpose. It is up to both the client and the design team to understand what that purpose is, and to determine the depth and the tone of voice that the written copy needs to communicate. Understanding what needs to be said, to whom and where it must be placed in the design, gives you the information needed to brief a copywriter to produce written content that is tailored to the UI's specific target audience. Happy and engaged users mean that the client will achieve their objectives more quickly.

It is important for the designer to know how much copy will be required, so they can accommodate that in the UI's design. Most UIs (except blogs and news sites/apps) do not need a great deal of text.

The art of copywriting

Copy must communicate what it needs to in a tone and at a level that the target audience will appreciate.
If it is not written in a concise manner, the reader may get confused and give up – it must be both scannable and readable. To explain this further, it may be best to separate this discussion into two components: copy as content, and copy as labels.

Any labels for icons, image captions, or headers and subheaders must be short. The choice of words used in labels should also be 'user facing' – using language the user will easily understand. Who wants to read a label stating 'return to level one', when 'home' is far friendlier and more inviting?

With body text, it is important to write short, concise sentences. Five or six sentences would form a satisfying paragraph length. Keep in mind that the first sentence of a paragraph is loaded with importance, and must keep the reader reading. The length of any body text is dependent on what needs to be communicated and where it will be displayed in the UI. If large amounts of copy are required, it should be split into short sections. In this way, the UI design can be optimized to deliver large amounts of written content, either through scrolling or splitting it across several screens or pages.

4.4

Semiotics is an underlying theory on which successful visual communication is built. It focuses on the connection between what you see (the signifier) and what it means (the signified). These two parts form a semiotic sign. The semiotics within design should be carefully considered; without a clear selection of visual components within a UI, miscommunication can occur. This section examines how semiotics works and how it can be applied within a UI to help create an aesthetic user experience.

The visual – more than just looks

According to the maxim, a picture is worth a thousand words. But which thousand words does an image suggest? An understanding of semiotic signs will help any designer to ensure that the visuals they select suggest the desired meaning to the viewer. Context is key to this, as there are many different ways with which to communicate meaning.

Any photograph, illustration, icon or UI layout has several layers of structure that can be read with semiotics. A visual signifier has structures that are conceptual, visual and textual. The interplay between these structures aids the viewer's perception of the sign. The viewer (user) then decodes the signified meaning through interpretation. How successfully this is done ultimately depends on the way the viewer deciphers the underlying signified meaning.

Semiotic terms (in a UI context)

Destination
interactive action in some form

Intention
what needs to be communicated and why

Message
the UI's various action calls or content areas

Noise
external interference of the transmission and receiving of a semiotic message

Receiver
the UI's user

Sender
the graphic designer

Sign
a visual that communicates specific meaning (the signifier and signified)

Signified
the meaning of the concept in the signifier

Signifier
a visual that represents a concept

Transmission
the typography, colour, written copy, multimedia, images, and visual affordances

www.sickcityclub.net

4.5
Sick City Club –
signifying 'attitude'
Sick City Club, a young band
from Birmingham (UK), needed
to project the right attitude to
their audience. Their website
UI signified this with stark
contrasts between black and
white, and various components.
All of these factors are individual
signifiers, but combined they
communicate an attitude
visually. www.sickcityclub.net

4.6
Tone of voice
The lengthening of the white
capital 'i' of city into the word
'sick' is sharpened by the
black 'i' of 'sick' being sheared
diagonally to form a point. The
typography contains strong
negative spaces and angles that
reinforce the tone of voice being
signified. The message here is
'urban' and 'risky'.

4.7
How visual components
signify meaning
The navigation is turned on its
side, invading the silhouetted
skyline. This is an example of
how the visual components
reinforce the idea of attitude and
edginess. Turning the navigation
forces the user to tilt their heads
to read the links, and reinforces
a signified meaning that can be
understood as being from an
alternative perspective.

Deciphering signified meanings

A photograph, illustration, icon or UI layout can suggest several differing meanings depending upon the context in which it is being interpreted. A designed visual is never neutral, and from a cultural perspective, it may suggest different meanings in different societies. Even within a single society the viewer (user) may make different social interpretations depending on their age, gender, class, religious or political beliefs, and so on.

In a semiotic sign there is always a sender of a 'message'. Within UI design this role rests with the graphic designer. The user of the interface is the recipient of the semiotic message, which is delivered by the designed visual. The message in a UI is the communication of the various action calls and content areas. By understanding semiotics as a means of interpreting the desired meaning of UI content, a designer can shape and accentuate the visual communication of the UI's messages.

With every decision made in the design of the interface, there is an *intention* to communicate (that is why the graphic designer is a visual communicator). What the message is depends on the content, the target users and the client. It may be the communication of the various action calls and content areas, or a 'cool' or 'corporate' or 'friendly' visual identity.

Transmission of meaning

Understanding semiotics will help you to clearly communicate a chosen message. The selection and crafting of the typography, colour, written copy, multimedia, images, and visual affordances allow the transmission of the message to the user. If the wrong typeface, colour or image is chosen, it could transmit a completely different message from the one you intended. Think about the door analogy again – the wrong shaped door handle may make someone pull instead of push.

Any interference between the transmission and receiving of a semiotic message is referred to as 'noise'. Semiotic noise within UI design can include several things. The UI's technology delivery platform may be too slow or too quick, preventing the signified semiotic message from being received in full. The display screen may not display colour in the desired way, and this may also interfere with the carefully crafted semiotics.

The destination of a signified semiotic message in a UI design will result in an action of some form. In a UI, this may be a successful call to action, such as a link being clicked, or it may be simply that the user locates the desired content amid a plethora of competing information. The visual examples in this section should help explain how semiotics in a UI works, by identifying the signifiers within the design and what they signify. By carefully selecting and shaping the semiotic signs, you are more likely to enable a successful aesthetic user experience.

4.8

"They have a
glittering, promising,
future ahead of them." ...WWW.NME.COM

How semiotics works

Sender > Intention > Message >
Transmission > Noise > Receiver > Destination

— Sean Hall, *This Means This, This Means
That* (2007, Laurence King)

4.8
The destination – content
The content copy is overlaid
in text boxes on the black
background, which contains
the band's videos played at
full screen. This band review
is stepped downwards across
three horizontal lines. These
lines visually suggest the five
staff lines used in musical
composition, and the stepping
of the quote across the lines
suggests musical notation.

The English language, although an international language, is not the only language to be used in a UI. Maybe native English-speakers are spoilt on the Web because most of the websites are written in English, but it is dangerous for a designer to believe this is the norm to universally design for. Many UIs, whether on the Web, an app on a phone, software on a PC, a DVD/BD or computer game, come in many languages. Many non-English speaking people want to read the content and navigation of a UI in their own language. A designer needs to seriously consider this, as the implications on designing an effortless aesthetic user experience could become costly if internationalization is ignored.

Language

The world has effectively grown smaller since the advent of air travel and, more recently, the explosion in digital communication. Within the context of westernized societies, designers from English-speaking nations can become blinkered and believe the population of the world all have the same wants and needs. However, although in English-speaking nations people read from left to right, this is not universal and differences such as this must be considered when creating a UI.

In languages using an *abjads* writing system (such as Hebrew and Arabic), the norm is to read from right-to-left; and languages represented through *logographic* writing systems (such as Chinese) can be read vertically or horizontally. Even within the languages used within Western countries that read left to right there are variations that a designer needs to be aware of. For example, word lengths in German are significantly longer than the equivalents in English.

4.9
Google doodles
Cultural differences can impact greatly on UI designs if the target users are from different cultures. Google has localized search engines in different languages. The Google doodles that feature over the search box also feature visual references to other cultures. This provides an international and inclusive feel to the web search.

English words average 5.10 characters in length, while German words average out at 6.26 characters. In comparison, a logographic language, such as Korean (represented using a Western alphabet), averages only 3.05 characters per word. If a paragraph of 300 words with 15 words per line is written in English, it takes up 19 lines. The same text, translated into German, will require 24 lines. In Korean, it will only fill 12 lines.

It should, therefore, be made clear before the information architecture phase of a project whether the UI design needs to accommodate multiple languages. This information should then inform how the layout of the UI design will be made and (from a typographical perspective) which language character sets will be used. By empowering the target users to access the UI in their chosen language, the user experience of the UI is improved without compromising the aesthetics.

Leonardo da Vinci's 553rd Birthday

Albert Einstein's 124th Birthday

Guy Fawkes Day
(an annual celebration in the UK)

Remembrance Day

St Patrick's Day

4.9

Father's Day

Reducing barriers through internationalization and localization

The games and entertainment industries have led the way for UI designers to understand how significant internationalization is. When a game or BD/DVD is loaded, there is often a prompt to select the required language. The selected language will then be displayed in the same UI design as the other languages would have been. An internationalized UI design is one that has been designed, from the outset, to accommodate a variety of language requirements and cultural differences.

Internationalization focuses on designing a UI for international access and reducing any barriers to accessibility in the design process. Decisions on supporting local, regional or culturally related references will be agreed at the beginning of the design phase. In doing this, the designer and developer will know how to format time and dates, calendars, currency, addresses/postal/zip codes, numbering, and so on.

Localization, on the other hand, is an adaptation of an existing UI into the language and culture of a specific target group. This involves more than merely adding translated copy to the UI and ensuring there is enough space to accommodate it. It may make it necessary to change the UI's colour palette, images and even icons. This is a lot of work, and can require a redesign of the aesthetic.

Therefore, when possible, it is better to plan for the UI to work cross-culturally very early on than to have to adapt it later. Not taking internationalization and localization into account when designing a UI will greatly diminish and disadvantage its aesthetic user experience.

Internationalization

'The design and development of a product, application or document content that enables easy localization for target audiences that vary in culture, region or language.'

Localization

'The adaptation of a product, application or document content to meet the language, cultural and other requirements of a specific target market (a 'locale').'

— *World Wide Web Consortium*

4.10
**Pflanzen Gegen Zombies –
multi-language design**
German and Chinese
editions of the popular
PopCap game *Plants vs.
Zombies*, accommodating
the longer German words
and the challenges of a
logographic language.

Role
User experience
designer, Standard
Life, UK

Experience
A UK-based
American UX
designer whose
clients have
included BP,
British Council,
Department of
Health, Epson,
Goldman Sachs,
Hilton, LEGO,
Merrill Lynch,
NHS, Royal & Sun
Alliance, Sprint,
UBS and Vodafone.

Web
www.linkedin.
com/pub/kristin-
kramer/0/10a/646

What does a user experience (UX) designer contribute to the interface design team?

The role entails a broad spectrum of things because a UX designer is involved in the design process from the beginning to the very end. They mediate primarily between the client objectives and user objectives. The reason they have to understand both of these is that half of the challenge of the job is being able to justify and rationalize why certain decisions have been made on behalf of the user.

A UX designer gets the client to articulate and prioritize their objectives. The client is paying for the design team's time and the interface has to help them make a return on their investment; so objectives and ways of measuring success go hand-in-hand. The UX designer evaluates the project at hand, understands any objective gaps and overlaps, and then comes up with a common set of design objectives.

Then they have to get the same thing from the users' perspective. What is their context of use? It is the experience of the user, how the page is laid out, what the key messages are, what gets visual prominence on the page, what's the call of action, and what does the user do next?

'Collaboration is a big deal – you don't just hand the project over from one phase to the next, because one person's input affects what the whole team is doing.'
– Kristen Kramer

Who has a stake in the design of a UI, beyond the end user?

The various stakeholders in developing an interface include the client, the developers, a copywriter, and a graphic designer. A UX designer has to be able to talk to all these people in their own technical languages, and go from broad concepts down into details. There is a lot of zooming in and out, so it helps to be very process driven. Flexibility is important, as UX designers chop and change their approach based on the resources and the time they have available. It's good to have constraints because otherwise, you won't know where to start.

When designing the user experience, how do you work with the developer and the graphic designer?

Everyone brings something to the table, so treat the graphic designer and developer as stakeholders. Consider them as equal collaborators. If there's written copy, or an image, or a video, or an interactive tool, it is all 'content'. Content is design. Collaboration is a big deal – you don't just hand the project over from one phase to the next, because one person's input affects what the whole team is doing.

That comes back to understanding the customer and understanding what the right solution is. The team needs to know where the user is coming from, and where they're going to go to next. More and more people are watching TV sitting there with their PC tablets or smartphones. There are stats floating around in the UK that say things like by 2015 mobile (smartphone and tablet) use will outstrip desktop use*. So it makes sense for the design team to try to think about design for mobile use first, so that everything else falls into place around that.

*Global Internet usage will more than double by 2015, and most of these users will be mobile (Boston Consulting Group, Mary Meeker, Kleiner Perkins, Morgan Stanley Research).

Content

The purpose of the interactive kiosk interface was not to inform the user, but to gather important information from them. This purpose was honestly stated so that the user knew what was required from them before they interacted with it. The content and written copy were crafted to ensure the user immediately understood what to do, and the visual communication encouraged them to commit to signing up to the skills competitions. The target users were 12–19 year olds, so the exhibition and kiosk's content needed to engage young people and make them want to associate themselves with the event.

The typography chosen helped brand the event and communicate a certain 'cool factor' to the target audience. Based upon a typeface called RITA, Purpose crafted a square and blocky typeface especially for the event. The exhibition was in the English language, so the choice of typeface worked well digitally in the kiosk interface as well as on all printed media, and as 3D word sculptures placed around the exhibition hall.

'The interface needed to be simple, engaging, on-brand with WorldSkills, and connect in the hall to a large video display'

**4.11
The WorldSkills
kiosk interface**
The kiosk interface has a simple five-stage process: the initial welcoming screen (1); the camera interface screen; the sign-up page (2); drop-down menus help the user to define themselves (in terms useful for the client); the profile is set and the information is displayed on the video screens (3).

**4.12
Copywriting WorldSkills**
The interface's copy is clear, succinct and very user-friendly. All the usual information labels are standardized, making these areas instantly familiar to the user.

4.12

Enter your name

First name...   Surname...

Your email address

Please enter...

Start your journey

I am...   Interested in...

■ I agree to the _privacy policy_   ■ I am over 16

Submit   Reset

I am...	Interested in...
A Future Competitor	Entering a competition
An Employer	Attending a competition in my area
A College or Training Provider	WorldSkills UK newsletters
A School	WorldSkills Team UK
An Alumni	

Semiotics

The design decisions behind the visual identity used in the kiosk interface can be deconstructed through examining the semiotics. Within the kiosk interface design, there are many signifiers and visual affordances that signify meaning. The bold, chunky display typeface used for 'I AM...' signifies the central theme of the exhibition – that it is the largest of its kind AND that the individual visitor is important. The diagonal blocks of colour help guide the eye to the white content areas, signifying the important parts of the screen.

The convention of buttons being embossed in their clickable state is followed, and this is borrowed very subtly in the use of purple and ochre on the right and underside of the white content areas. This combination 'pushes out' the white content areas toward the user, signifying that attention is required in these sections. The input fields and calls for action are coloured red (the most emotive action colour), with white text, for ultimate contrast. This signifies that these areas are active and demand attention. A photograph is required for registration and the human shaped grey silhouette signifies this.

Call for action and reward

The visitor experience that the kiosk interface communicated was one of 'inclusion and participation' within a huge exhibition. The user of the UI was presented with a simple, achievable task. During each of the five interactive steps, users knew exactly what was happening and what their next action needed to be. As a reward for registering, their photograph was displayed on the large video display in the large exhibition hall welcoming them to the event.

4.13

4.13
The semiotics of WorldSkills
Within the visual communication of the interface, the semiotics operates on a subconscious level, guiding the user. (1) From "I AM..." the diagonal colour bars direct the user to the two areas that need completing. (2) The two input areas emerge from the background through the use of the purple and the ochre. (3) The blank human shape (coloured red for emphasis) gives a subtle visual affordance that a photograph is required. (4) The input areas and action calls are all coded red with white text. Buttons conform to W3 web standards, and the reset button is in a neutral grey.

Premise

This exercise focuses on semiotics, including the user's point of view, the ways in which written copy communicates, and cultural contexts. In particular, we will focus on deconstruction and interpretation skills as you will need to put yourself in the first-person perspective of a user looking at a UI for the first time. This exercise can be repeated and adapted until it becomes second nature.

You can use this exercise for any UI, but we will use Whitespace's interface for The Scotch Malt Whisky Society as an example.

Outcomes

This exercise will help inform your visual communication decisions through deconstructing the semiotics of an existing UI. It can be applied to any UI, and it is recommended that you repeat it using different types of UI. Deconstruction is only part of the process. You need to learn from the deconstruction and use what you've learned. This exercise can be combined with the exercise at the end of Chapter 2 to give you some fundamental skills to help you design future interfaces.

**4.14–4.17
Deconstruction**
To keep this exercise simple, we will deconstruct a single UI screen. Follow the instructions in the exercise overleaf and refer back to the images on this page.

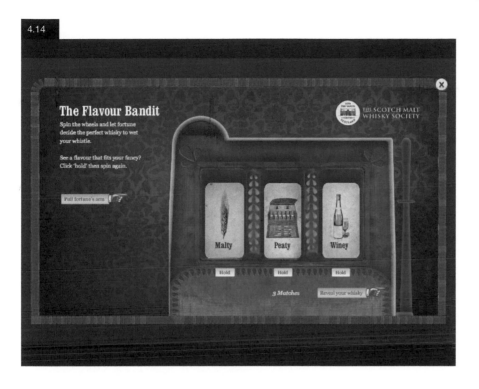

4.14

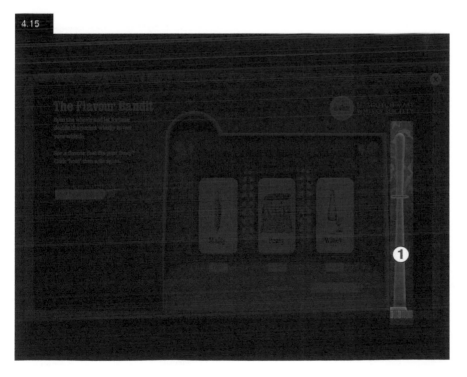

4.15

4.16

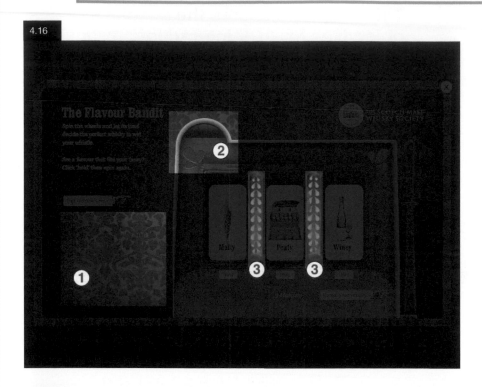

4.17

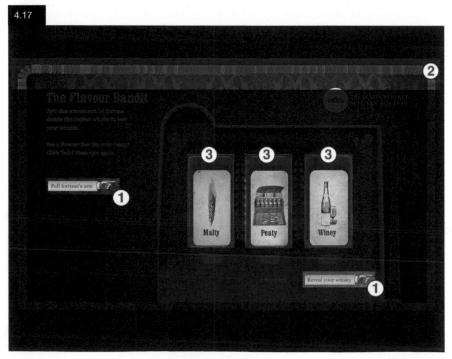

Exercise

This exercise works best through discussion, so feel free to share your answers, but it can also be conducted alone. The deconstruction process itself is fairly simple. The challenge is interpretation – looking and thinking – to see what the semiotic messages are and how the semiotic sign is constructed. You are in the position of a user who doesn't know what the design team's intention was – only how the design of the UI communicates itself visually.

The exercise is split into three parts:

1. The semiotic signs

Look at the whole interface.

— What is the purpose of this UI?

— Who is its target audience?

— Why does it look this way?

— How do I recognize the available calls to action?

2. Isolating the signifiers

Identify visual elements that you think may be semiotic signs. Group the signifiers that you think may be suggesting the same message (images 4.15–4.17 have already done this for you).

Take each isolated signifier group and ask the following:

— Why is the signifier that shape?

— Why is the signifier that colour?

— Why is the signifier created using typography/an illustration/a photograph (or a combination of these)?

3. Finding the signified (semiotic meaning)

This is where the fun begins.
Look at image 4.14.

— Why has this colour palette been chosen?

— What does this illustration say that a photograph wouldn't?

Look at image 4.15.

— There is a call to action at (1). How do we know this through the visual communication?

Now look at image 4.16.

— (1) What does the choice of wallpaper and the lighting on it signify?

— (2) Does this detail signify a call to action or is it simply a part of the illustration without any function? Discuss.

— (3) What do these details signify?

Finally look at image 4.17.

— (1) These two calls to action are visually communicated in a particular way, so what does this sign communicate beyond the obvious?

— (2) What does this choice of border communicate?

— (3) Why use old engraved images on the display? What is the deeper meaning of this for the user?

Collaborating with the developer

Great UI designs, and great user experiences, require the designer and the developer to collaborate. This chapter will explore positive ways in which the graphic designer can optimize their communication with the developer when designing an interface. Designing for modularity will be examined both in theory and in practice, with examples from real design jobs.

An interview with designer/developer Alan Bridge and a case study on Creative Griffin will show how the graphic design of the UI is prepared for coding by the developer. This working relationship with the developer will be championed, and the end of chapter exercise will give you an opportunity to practice designing with modularity in mind.

'Designing for modularity' means identifying and deconstructing patterns of use in a single UI design. Any design process begins in creative chaos and the UI design solution develops through an iterative period of complexity until a suitable outcome is designed. So designing for modularity is about streamlining (not homogenizing) the designer's creativity, and building a design system of repeatable assets for reuse.

This streamlining of assets for reuse means that the developer will only need to write the code that describes an asset once, and then reuse that code time and time again wherever that asset appears in the UI. This improves the user experience as reused code throughout the UI makes loading times quicker. Of course, this doesn't mean that every asset used in the interface design will be repeatable in the UI.

A rationale for designers

It isn't enough to make a great looking UI design in Photoshop, Fireworks, Illustrator or even InDesign as a composite ('comp') – the graphic designer has to think modularly as they make design decisions. By deconstructing and identifying repeatable and non-repeatable design assets, the designer can create a suitable aesthetic experience, so that the design communicates simplicity of use to the user.

As a designer, you will be creating the UI design in a digital file that will be handed over to the developer. This file will show each page of the UI with the assets composited within a grid. This is called a 'comp' file in designer's language. If a grid is being used then part of the work of modularization has already begun. Photoshop PSD files are commonly used, but as we have already seen, this is not the only design software.

If each page variant of the UI shares that same grid and visual hierarchy, then assets on a single page or across the UI will conform to agreed size ratios for assets (agreed by the team). If an asset repeats itself across the UI design more than once, it can be modularized. This helps the designer to define pixel-perfect assets and the spatial relationships between them. In turn this helps the developer.

Designing with modularity in mind does not mean that a graphic designer's initial creativity and innovation need to be restricted (a common fear about translating designs into code). It allows for clearer communication between the designer and developer, and begins to create a common visual language between the two, which leads to good design practice.

5.1

5.2

5.1
Same UI, different platforms
Depending on the platform detected by the code, a different version of the UI will be displayed. Each selected version of the UI will be optimized for that platform and will display the content differently while maintaining a common visual identity across the versions using modularity of assets.

5.2
Code-controlling structure
In this example, the source code for the HTML structure of the website is overlaid on top of the content. The CSS that controls the styling and the JavaScript that controls the interactivity are not shown. The layout and structure suggest which elements are content and which are assets.

To demonstrate the importance of communication between the developer and the designer, we will look at a provocative little scenario to illustrate how miscommunication arises between them. We have previously discussed first-person perspectives in the context of understanding where the user is coming from (see page 114). Now a first-person perspective will be used to show how the designer and developer do not perceive the same things when they see each other's work.

As a graphic designer, if you were given a page of code by a developer and told to design a UI from that, it would be difficult. It wouldn't make sense to you, as that is not the language you work in. Even though the code describes things that you would recognize, such as hierarchy, headings, colour and text, it is presented in a form you might not currently understand. Until you've been trained in programming it appears as gobbledegook to you.

Now reverse that scenario.

If a developer is given a Photoshop PSD comp file by a designer and told to code it, similar problems arise as developers see the UI in the context of markup code. They need more information than a Photoshop file from the designer. If the PSD file doesn't help the developer understand the spatial relationships of (and between) design elements, or the intended pixel margins, then it is just pretty pictures. The developer will have to interpret the picture to understand what the designer needs them to code.

Designing for modularity helps to break down the 'gobbledegook' and 'pretty pictures' prejudices, and develops a visual communication language between the two specialisms that plays to the strengths of each.

'Copy, art, typography — and technology — are the bones of a project, where design and development are the joints and skin that connect and hold together the parts. When all of these elements fit together well, you essentially have design and development working together as the support structure for the user experience and overarching concept, the so-called "living entity".'
– Cassie McDaniel (based on a quote from Paul Rand), *Smashing Magazine*

The benefits of designing modularly

Designing modularly has many benefits and is a win:win:win design methodology. Ultimately, other than affording faster load times, the process ensures that there is a consistency in the UI's visual hierarchy. This is achieved through clearer communication within the design team, with the designer maintaining control over the design without being at the expense of the developer. This creates a stronger working relationship in the team and a better experience for the user.

The designer wins as they get to design an interface aesthetic that they know will be translatable into code. The developer wins, as they will get the design in a way that makes their job of coding it much easier. Finally, the user gets an interface that has been built mostly of modular assets and is fast loading. The users win because they don't realize this, but get a quick-loading aesthetic user experience in the use of the interface.

That is why designers and developers need a good collaborative iterative dialogue at each stage of UI design, in which the developer needs to communicate to the designer what they need. What these are and how a designer provides them will be discussed in more detail later in the chapter. First, we'll define what modular assets are.

Main benefits of modularity

For the designer

— Controlling the process of designing from complexity to simplicity

— Ensuring the consistency of the visual hierarchy

— Refining design details to streamline into repeatable assets

— Refocusing on the designer's crafting of the visual communication

For the developer

— Clearer communication with the designer

— Common visual language

— Reusable system to streamline coding

For the user

— Faster load times

— Consistency of visual hierarchy

— Consistency of aesthetic experience across display platforms

If you work within a grid with modular asset sizes, then you will clarify a lot of the detail the developer needs. Specific placement of the assets in the gridded design will allow for specific location information that the developer can translate into code. Dimensions of assets will be standardized, and their position in the comp layout will provide precise data, such as column widths, asset width and height and x and y position from top left. Once the digital comp file of the design has been layered, grouped and labelled, it is ready to be passed to the developer or development team. But which assets will become modular and coded for reuse?

Which assets are modular?

So what are repeatable and non-repeatable assets in a design comp? To get us started, here are two examples of non-repeatable features that cannot be coded as modular.

1. Variable content, such as the written copy of body text or an image, cannot be modular (although the container that holds and formats the text or image can be).

2. Non-standard dimensioned assets require specific code to be written that cannot be reused. When used sparingly in the visual communication, they can have more impact on the user – especially when attention needs to be directed to a particular piece of content.

By ensuring that most of the design's assets, such as text and image boxes, navigation components (buttons), rounded corners and lines, conform to modular size ratios and to the underlying gridded columns, they can become reusable in the coding of the design. For example, the structure of global or contextual navigation will be modular even though within the module the wording on a button may change as the code can easily be written to overlay different words on top of each module. This is great for both internationalization and localization of the UI as the code can control which language is displayed depending on who the user is.

5.3

16px unit 976px page width

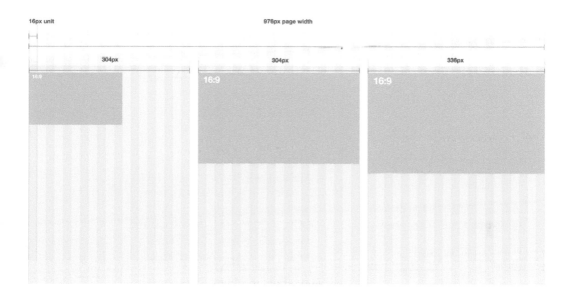

304px 304px 336px

16:9 16:9 16:9

5.4

submit >

click here >

more >

5.3
**Image box and image
size ratios**
Agreeing a ratio of image
sizes allows the designer
to be creative with placing
images, having the knowledge
that the developer will create
reusable pieces of code to
use throughout a UI that may
contain hundreds of images.
The image boxes shown here
are all in landscape orientation,
but it is equally straightforward
to set a reusable image ratio for
portrait display.

5.4
Modular components
Parts of your design can be
reused elsewhere in the UI.
This includes things like text
and image boxes, navigation
components (buttons), rounded
corners, lines etc. These are
referred to as 'modules' and
they fit to the underlying grid.

What the developer needs

The comp file needs to remain unflattened, but it is good practice to also supply additional guidance to the developer. It is useful to make a PDF page layout spec sheet as a style guide of the UI design (the BBC GEL style guide is an example of this, see page 71). This will be a flattened version of the UI design and will generally show:

— each page variant

— RGB values of the key colours used

— additional information on typography and asset sizes

— how each interactive state in the UI visually works.

Providing a PDF page layout spec sheet for the developer is not compulsory, and there isn't a standard format for making one. They can often improve communication between the designer and developer, preventing miscommunication which can cause significant delays in the design process. If the designer doesn't make something like this available to the developer, there are very likely to be problems with accuracy. With a little extra time spent labelling layers, grouping states and providing reference and RGB colour guides, many little problems can be avoided early in coding the UI.

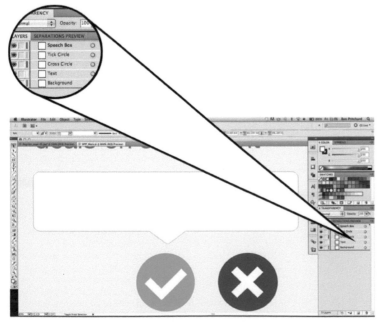

5.5

5.5
Layered interactive states
Clearly layering, grouping and labelling interactive states in the assets will help the developer understand both the context and how the visual affordance (the clues to its function and use) will work in order to code it.

5.6
PDF reference guide
Once the developer begins to separate the unflattened digital file into coded modules, it is easy to lose sight of how it will all function as a whole. A PDF reference guide shows how the assets will work. There is no definitive template for an RGB colour reference guide (see page 81). The requirements should be agreed between the designer and the developer, and will vary in detail depending on the project and team. In its basic form, it is a list of the colours used in the design in RGB values and/or hexadecimal values.

Case study
WorldSkills interactive kiosk

Project
**Using the
WorldSkills
London 2011
event as a
catalyst, Purpose
were presented
with the challenge
of how to register
and capture data
for more than
5,000 potential
new recruits for
the 2012 skills
competitions.**

Design team
**Purpose, London,
UK**

Client
WorldSkills UK

Objectives and expected outcomes

Design company Purpose were commissioned to create a visitor experience for WorldSkills UK's vocational training exhibition. The client's objective was to raise the awareness of Europe-wide vocational training at their London exhibition, and then after the event. They hoped to attract an audience of 150,000 to the exhibition, and get the young visitors to identify and associate with specific career routes.

More than 200,000 visitors attended the event, and around 5,000 of these would need to register on the day for the skills competitions. To facilitate this, Purpose designed an interactive kiosk. The interface needed to be simple, engaging, on-brand with WorldSkills, and connect in the hall to a large video display. Purpose developed a fun and engaging five-step interaction to capture each visitor's details and their photograph.

5.6

Creative Griffin*

Primary Logo

3.5%

Safe Zone

4mm of space all the way around at all sizes

3.5%

35%

19mm

36%

29%

93%

158mm

ALTERNATIVE LOGO VERSIONS

Secondary Logo Style

Minimum Logo Width

Social Profile Images

FONTS USED IN LOGOTYPE

ITC Lubalin Graph BT

The quick red fox jumps over the lazy brown dog
The quick red fox jumps over the lazy brown dog
The quick red fox jumps over the lazy brown dog
The quick red fox jumps over the lazy brown dog
The quick red fox jumps over the lazy brown dog
The quick red fox jumps over the lazy brown dog

COLOUR SPECIFICATIONS - Black and white

C0 M0 Y0 K100	C0 M0 Y0 K40	C0 M0 Y0 K30	C0 M0 Y0 K0
#000000	#b5b5b5	#c9c9c9	#ffffff

COLOUR SPECIFICATIONS - Colour

C100 M0 Y0 K0	C0 M0 Y100 K0	C0 M0 Y100 K20	C0 M0 Y0 K0
#009ae3	#f9f200	#d6d100	#ffffff

For a developer to make sense of the design comp file they need the digital file in unflattened layers, with clear labelling and grouping of different interactive states into sub-layers. All the navigation assets can be grouped together (with sub-layers for specific parts or contextual navigation). In these sub-layers the interactive states of every call-to-action design element need to be appropriately labelled (for example, print-btn_up, print-btn_down, print-btn_hover).

By structuring and grouping the assets logically in layers, it will be clearer to the developer where to find the assets so they can isolate each one and write the code to display it.

It is good practice to layer and label with descriptive terms as your design comp progresses, as it makes it easy for anyone to see what is repeatable and non-repeatable, interactive and non-interactive.

Integrating modularity into your workflow will help the UI to display more fluidly by ensuring a solid connection between the design and the code. It is an adaptable methodology, which can be applied to small or large interface projects, helping the interface to respond to whichever platform it is being displayed on.

Deconstructing the design

So, how do you introduce modularity into your design?

Begin by viewing all the UI design's page variants side-by-side and highlighting which assets are repeated and which are not. This highlighting can be done on screen, but it is more effective if the page variants are printed out. Using this approach will enable you to look at the design with fresh eyes and identify which assets will be modular (see image 5.7). Using different colours to indicate the different types of modular assets will aid identification.

If you've designed a consistent visual hierarchy for the UI with global and contextual navigation, it should become obvious which assets repeat on each page variation. Highlight these buttons (orange boxes), text boxes (blue boxes), image boxes (green boxes) or other repeated elements (yellow and red boxes).

Once all the UI repeated modular assets have been identified and highlighted, it is easy to see which assets are not repeated. You will then need to group and label the layers in the digital comp file, making it clear which are modular and which are not repeated. Finally, you can compile the PDF page layout spec sheet as a style guide ready for the developer.

5.7
Highlighting modular assets
The assets that are repeated should be highlighted to draw attention to them. Once the different modular assets have been identified, ensure that the comp file groups the assets and their interactive states together. Labels should be meaningful and clearly describe what the layer contains to communicate to the developer what they need to code.

Role
Website Designer/
Developer,
Creative Griffin,
UK

Experience
Journey from
graduate to
professional
designer/developer

Web
www.
creativegriffin.
co.uk

Can you give me a picture of your journey into becoming a UI front-end designer?

I began on night courses at my local college. Then I gained a place on a BA design degree. On the degree, I started working on the more visual side of interaction – the graphic design. Once I graduated I worked at a printer as a graphic designer. I oversaw all their digital work because they were all litho printers. I was with them for just over a year or so and got introduced to another job – website design.

How did you find the transition from designing for print to interactive?

I had to step up my game. I had to learn CSS (I got the basics in three days) and I learned more HTML. Since I started, I've learned PHP and now I'm getting my head around HTML5. But I also learned more about the process of how a site should be made. I've been telling all my clients that all their competitors are just a click away. So the design has to be easy and keep the users thinking *'this is where I'm going – this is what I want'* because at any moment, they can click on Google in the top right of the browser and they're gone.

'The design has to be easy and keep the users thinking *"this is where I'm going – this is what I want"'*
– Alan Bridge

How has understanding the development side helped you as a website designer?

As a designer, you used to rely on images for website backgrounds, titles and textures; images can take up anything from a couple of megabytes or just a few kilobytes. The original CSS was just the basics of 'square', 'colour', 'background colour'. Now, CSS3 is basically graphic design in code. CSS3 styles the website and makes it easy for file sizes to be really small. It's only a couple of kilobytes now and it makes the sites load very quickly.

I structure all my sites in PHP, with HTML inside. If you have just an HTML site and you have ten pages that are all the same layout, you're going to have to make an HTML file for each one of those pages. With PHP it's easier; you only have to make one file as a structural container so it's uploading the same file every time. The only thing it's changing each time is the content.

What is your technique for deciding which assets will be modular?

I generally start by going through the brief and then go to the client with a web design idea made in InDesign. We will discuss what they want on the home page, how the other pages would look and how they want the user to go through the UI to get the information. I don't make it in Photoshop because I find that I can move things around a lot more easily with InDesign. For example, if you make a square with a gradient in Photoshop and then decide to scale it up, it would pixelate.

I then take the InDesign file and I spend a good couple of hours going through the design, going through each page (sometimes I'll print it off if it's a really complex site). I'll start with a marker pen and I'll circle saying *'that's CSS,' 'this is an image,'* etc. Where it has to be an image – it has to be an image. If I can do the same thing in CSS3 then I'll do that, purely because it keeps the file size down. I'll just deconstruct the design in that way, ready to code.

Project
getmy
loanfeesback.com

Design team
Creative Griffin,
www.
creativegriffin.
co.uk

Client
Consolidate
Me Ltd

Preparing to modularize

Creative Griffin was commissioned to build a website for a new business venture in the consumer financial service compensation market.
In preparation for the launch of getmyloanfeesback.com, the graphic designer worked closely with the developer to break down the client's brief into a workable website idea.

Both discussed the pros and cons of the aesthetic and functional decisions to ensure that the proposed design suited both the client and the target user. The visual communication had to communicate a friendly, accessible and trustworthy compensation service for the consumer. At the same time, to fulfil the client's needs, the website also had to clearly communicate enough information to facilitate the consumer placing a compensation claim via the website.

5.8
The website idea in InDesign
The proposed design of the website is first constructed within Adobe InDesign software. The UI elements are easier to scale and adjust. Each asset is contained in its own layer, with descriptive labels, to explain them to the developer.

5.9
Website design
ready to modularize
The website has several page variations in its design, these are printed out actual size so that the modular elements can be highlighted.

Once a design idea was agreed, which worked for both the user and the client, the designer and developer began to work on the UI. The designer began putting a design comp together, using Adobe InDesign as his software of choice to lay out the design to a grid. He ensured that all the assets in the comp were grouped and labelled descriptively, ready for the developer to slice up and code.

This website design had several page variations to the set layout. The designer took time (once the layouts had been designed) to check to see what would or would not be modular assets. By looking at all the page variations together (in this case he printed them out), he could examine the assets across all the pages at the same time. This made it easier to spot repeated assets.

5.8

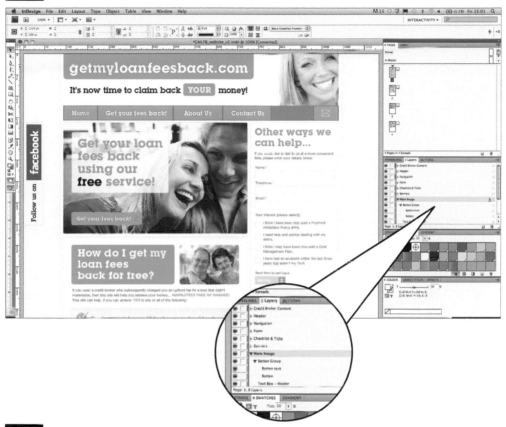

5.9

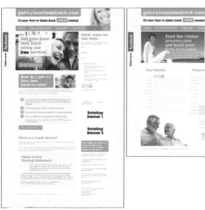

Highlighting modularity

Using a marker pen on the printed-out page variants, the designer spent some time going through each page of the website design. He first highlighted all the obvious assets that repeated across the pages. The lines and radii of the written content, images, media boxes would be set by the code anyway. But the boxes themselves fell into different categories. These would also be modular and could be coded once by the developer so they were highlighted as modular.

Some assets repeated just within a single page, and these were also highlighted as being modular. Although the designer was experienced and designed the UI with modularity in mind, it was good for him to look over a design that he is so familiar with with fresh eyes. While highlighting the modular assets, he was thinking about his design and what the developer could code once and reuse. He kept thinking, 'That asset is repeated and could be coded in CSS.' or 'This asset is not repeated. It may need to be an image with its own code.'

Where the asset was not repeated, it was highlighted and labelled as non-modular. All this information helped the developer to assess what type of approach to take to coding the website, which assets could be coded once and reused, and which assets would need bespoke code to be written.

Deconstructed and ready for the developer

Once the designer had completed the audit of his design for modular assets, he labelled them in the layers of the InDesign file. Along with the digital file, the designer also provided the developer with a reference guide, including the relevant RGB colours. This helped the developer to slice up the design and code more effectively. At this stage of the design process, the designer and developer maintained a dialogue on the modularity of design to ensure the website's successful completion.

Once coded and ready to test, the visual communication of the UI's design remained unchanged. A user would not be aware of which assets were reused and which were unique to the page. They were only aware that the website downloaded the assets quickly from the server, ready for them to make a claim.

5.10

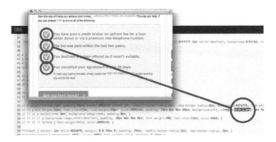

5.11

5.12

5.10
The modular components in the code
Once the modular components have been identified and labelled for the developer, they can be coded. The final design appears in the browser as a fully cohesive design (inset), but on examination of the code it is clear what is coded as CSS and what are images.

5.11
Example of design assets that will become modular
The elements on each page that are consistently repeated can become modular and controlled by the code. Other elements that may only be repeated on a single page can also be controlled by the code.

5.12
Example of design assets that are not repeated
The parts of the design that obviously aren't repeated won't be modular. Images, although they are visually different, can fit into modular sizes of image boxes. That way, the image can be different, but conforms to a visual hierarchical scale of regular image sizes. The image box can be controlled by the code, while the image inside can vary.

Premise

This chapter has discussed modularity of assets and how designers structure their comp files of the UI design ready for the developer. This exercise will help you to begin to think about designing with modularity in mind, and to consolidate it practically. Its aim is to deconstruct several variant pages of a UI design and highlight which assets are repeated and which are not. It will help you streamline your design using modular assets and prepare you for working with a developer.

You can use a UI design of your own for this exercise. Choose one that has several page variants. If you can partner up with someone to do this exercise, then swap your UI designs with him or her. Doing so will overcome your familiarity with your own UI design, making it easier to spot reusable assets. *Use a UI design where you have the digital file with at least two page variants in an un-flattened layered file.* The focus is on preparing a static design for a developer to code, and not adding the interactivity to the design.

Outcomes

This exercise in modularity gets you to examine the design decisions you take in the creation of the visual communication of a UI, so that you can streamline your design using modular assets where possible. It should help prepare you for working with a developer, and can be undertaken even if you currently don't have any developers to work with. It can be repeated as often as you like with different UI designs, but the highlighting of the assets is not the end of the task. Ensure that you also get used to labelling the layers in your design software as you go. The more you think about designing for modularity, the quicker you will make it a normal part of your design process.

The exercise is not suitable for a UI built directly in authoring software, such as Adobe Dreamweaver or Autodesk's Scaleform.

Exercise

Part 1: Scanning the UI design page variants

Print out the selection of page variants from your design comp file at 100 per cent.

Place each printed UI page variant side by side so you can compare them.

Identify which assets in the design are repeated across the page variants.

Identify any assets in the design that are repeated only on one page.

With a coloured marker, highlight these repeated assets.

With a different colour marker, highlight any assets that are not repeated.

Part 2: Grouping and labelling the assets in the digital file

Back in the digital comp file:

— Ensure that you have the asset layers clearly labelled with descriptive terms.

— Group any assets that should be together (for example, group navigation, group text boxes, group images), maintaining the integrity of the hierarchy of layers to prevent breaking the design.

— Ensure that any interactive states are also clearly labelled and grouped.

— Identify which groups are modular in nature and which will contain non-repeated assets.

Part 3: Preparing the reference guides

Now that the comp file has been optimized for the developer:

— Create a PDF version of the UI design showing each page variant. Also show how any interactive states on that page will look (such as up, down, hover), and annotate where necessary to explain this interaction.

— Name each page (Home page, Contact etc).

— Create an RGB colour reference guide showing the colours used in the design.

Augmenting human capabilities through interfaces

In this final chapter, the discussion will turn from the skills graphic designers need and the time at which to apply them, to future technological innovations that may impact on how interfaces are designed. We have looked at the change from WIMP interfaces to post-WIMP interfaces. Now, the implications of post-WIMP interfaces on the graphic designer will be explored.

The three technologies that will be discussed are QR codes, mobile augmented reality and touch screen. However, the focus will remain on how the designer can create an aesthetic user experience. Therefore, as the book comes to a close, the human user remains central to how a graphic designer visually communicates the UI design. It will end with an interview with Kate Ho on the multi-touchscreen Macallan Microsoft Surface at Schiphol Airport by Whitespace.

QR (quick response) codes are all around us – in homes, towns and cities around the world. But not everyone notices them or understands what they do. The QR code is a barcode with the capacity to hold tens of thousands of bits of information, and acts as a shortcut to web-based content from the physical world. This is where print meets the digital interactive world, as the code is a printed square that can be found on posters, leaflets, labels, books, magazines or any conceivable object. The QR code is scanned with an app on a smartphone that takes the user to related web-based data. The data types that a QR code can connect to include calendars, v- or e-cards, email addresses, geo-locations, phone numbers, URLs, e-tickets and surveys.

Quick response through visual communication

The QR code has a direct relevance to graphic designers, as it acts like a bridge between print and digital. These are two realms that the designer must have skills and training in. The QR code itself is a mini-interface between these two realms, and therefore needs careful consideration within the design process. The design team needs to safeguard the integrity of the data contained in the barcode, and ensure that whatever web-based destination it points the user toward is mobile-friendly.

The colour and contrast of the barcode on its background needs to be optimized, otherwise a QR reader will have trouble translating it. The team must ensure that the resolution and printed size are suitable and that the underlying grid is usable. There are a number of web-based code generators (Kaywa and Unitag are two) that will convert a data type to a QR code. But the code itself doesn't have to be utilitarian and merely black on white.

Graphic designer Jim Divine has pioneered branding QR codes that visually communicate the end destination of the link. He describes this branding of a QR code as a 'CyberLogo'. The skilful combination of an illustration or graphic into the barcode, while maintaining the required formatting, patterns of position, alignment and timing, can be very striking. Branding QR codes in such a fashion aids identification for the user, thereby increasing the chances of them scanning it. However, as always, less is more. If the QR code is overused, its impact and usefulness will be diminished.

6.1

6.2

6.3

6.1
CyberLogo
Graphic designer Jim Divine has developed the possibilities of embedding a branded visual identity within the barcoding information in a QR code. This 'CyberLogo' adds a whole new level of visual communication to the QR code by indicating where the code will take you.

6.2
What does QR do?
QR codes can be printed as stickers, or directly onto an item. It can then connect the user to a range of web-based information and control. Background information to the item may be available as an audio or video file, or the act of scanning the barcode could interact within a multimedia experience.

6.3
How QR works
The QR code is a square barcode. In three corners are squares that help the QR reader app position itself to decode (1). A smaller square in the bottom right-hand corner helps align the reader (2). The distribution of smaller jagged splotches contains the digitized information that connects to the Web (3).

Transportation from ink to digital

For the QR code to transport the user from print to the Web, they must have a smartphone with the right app and a camera to read the code. It doesn't matter whether the smartphone is iOS or Android, Blackberry or Windows, as they all have their own QR apps. What does matter is the content that the QR leads to and how it is presented – it needs to be suitable for display on a small screen. This is important, as otherwise the user will not have a good experience and may be put off scanning any future QR codes.

The QR code itself can be used in much more exciting ways. The barcode is generated as a graphic artefact than can be scaled (although not too small). Some researchers, such as Dr Oli Mival of Edinburgh Napier University, are exploring new ways in which codes can be embedded into a physical environment. These QR codes may be sculptural or carved, and yet remain readable to a QR app interfacing with web-based content specific to the relevant geographic location. This development makes a connection between the QR code and augmented reality.

6.4
QR in the environment
In principle, a QR code doesn't necessarily have to be printed; it could be structural within an environment. As long as the required barcoding data patterns of position, alignment, timing and data and error correction keys are translated across to the 3D-sculptured version it can still operate. The user of the QR reading app would have to stand further away from this to align the reader to the code.

6.5
QR meets AR
The significance of QR codes within a specific environment means contextual information can be coded into a location. This could unlock such things as video stories of a particular event which happened in that location. This is where the potential of QR codes makes a transition into augmented reality (AR).

6.4

6.5

AR STORYTELLING

Augmented Reality
Fiducial Marker

Another technology that may come to revolutionize how people interact digitally with the world around them is augmented reality (AR). It may be the next big thing between the interfacing of print and digital. AR is a technology that blurs the digital world with the real world by digitally overlaying a level of additional information onto what can be seen. This is currently done using a digital device, such as a smartphone. It enhances the experience of a real-world environment in real time. But effective AR visualization requires the careful application of visual communication principles.

Overlaying reality

AR is closer to the real world than the purely computer-generated virtual reality (VR). AR, using the camera in a smartphone and an app, essentially augments (increases) the real-world environment of the user by superimposing digital detail in real time. This information may be graphical, textual, audio or video in nature. In theory, whatever the camera points at, the AR app will add extra digital information layers accessed from the Web, which are contextual to the GPS position of the user.

Currently, the technology is still fairly rudimentary, but workable. Apart from a digital device to view it on (a smartphone), AR needs three components to successfully function:

— A marker to trigger the AR layered information

— Software to process the marker and deliver the content

— An interface to bring the three components of marker, software and content together to be accessed by the user.

This form of digital interface is more dynamic than anything currently experienced on the Web or on a smartphone app. This means that the visual communication of the layered information needs to accommodate a variety of dynamic content. In respect to handheld AR devices, such as smartphones with AR apps (like Layar in The Netherlands), the interface is constrained by the current restrictions of camera quality, screen size, resolution and data download speeds.

Within the screen, the AR interface will need to display the real-time environment in which the AR marker(s) sits, and then dynamically overlay a display of additional information drawn from the Web. Planning how this information will be displayed offers both exciting new opportunities to the graphic designer and new problems to overcome.

6.6

Future of Social Networking with Augmented Reality
Concept investigation by Matthew Buckland (matthewbuckland.com) and Philip Langley (@royalalien) of 20fourlabs.com

Future of Social Networking with Augmented Reality
Concept investigation by Matthew Buckland (matthewbuckland.com) and Philip Langley (@royalalien) of 20fourlabs.com

Future of Social Networking with Augmented Reality
Concept investigation by Matthew Buckland (matthewbuckland.com) and Philip Langley (@royalalien) of 20fourlabs.com

6.6
AR and social networking
These concept designs, made by Mathew Buckland and Philip Langley, explore how AR may impact on social networking in the future. They show the amount of overlaid data, accessed in real time, that may be required. This demonstrates a problem with AR that needs resolving with regard to functionality, visual communication and usability. Too much information overlaid at any one time will reduce the communication, not enough and the user will miss out. The design team needs to design for the Goldilocks (just right) solution, through experimentation and user testing.

6.7

6.8

The designer in the world

For the design team in general, and the graphic designer in particular, the display of content aggregated from the Web adds a new level of complexity to the design of interfaces; as the dynamic overlay of graphics, text and information over an image of the environment requires sensitivity. The visual examples of AR featured in this section are all essentially prototypes to show the potential of AR. Companies, such as Layar and Wikitude, are evolving the handheld AR experience on smartphones in a much more accessible way.

Like QR codes, the full impact of AR won't be felt until the general population of users feel the need for it. As Dr Sandor states, it's not until everyone can access it on their smartphones, and then find a use for it in their everyday life, that it will truly become as embedded into normal twenty-first-century life as touch screens and texting have. Notwithstanding this, it is still important for graphic designers to consider and plan ways to successfully visually communicate such an AR interface.

6.7
Connectedness
The connectedness between the user and a communicated message will evolve in many new ways. One such way was evidenced at the *One Giant Pledge Event* in 2012 in New York. It used AR to encourage families to eat one more vegetable a day through an oath made to the Jolly Green Giant himself.

6.8
New York Subway app
This AR app by acrossair is for locating NY Subway stations. If you hold the phone flat, all of the New York Subway lines are displayed. When the phone is tilted upwards, the nearest stations are overlaid on the screen in relation to the location and view. The AR interface loads in real time and displays directions, distance and lines available at the nearest stations.

Android, iOS, Blackberry and Windows mobile operating systems have all helped people to embrace the new touch-screen world. Since Apple launched the iPhone and opened up the market, smartphones and tablets are now outstripping sales of desktop PCs. It is therefore crucial for UI designers to remain up to date with advances in this technology, and this section will help you explore some design implications of touch.

Technology innovates and evolves faster than any book could be updated to cover it. As soon as technology is written about, it is out of date. Thankfully, this is not a book about technology; it is about designing interfaces for people to use. We, as human beings, evolve far more slowly than technology. Therefore, the capabilities of humans remain the same, they just need to adapt to a new way of working with a new tool. And that is all that touch-screen technology is – a new tool.

6.9

UI under glass

All digital technologies, in some way, help augment human capabilities. But we still use our hands and fingers (if we are able-bodied) to manipulate the tools we use. The tools may now be digital, but our hands and fingers are not. Our hands hold things, grasp things, and cup things. Our fingertips are covered in nerve endings, densely grouped, and they feed information to our brains for interpretation.

With touch-screen UIs, our interactions are more directly manipulated than with WIMP UIs. But we only really sense the feel of glass when we swipe or press the screen. It can therefore be said that the UI is 'under glass'; whereas with desktops we were separated from the content by the mouse and pointer. With touch screens we're now that bit closer to the interaction, but tantalizingly still not quite 'in' the interaction. The current designs of touch-screen UIs utilize the human finger and thumb in gestures to access and interact with the content. What is still missing from the interaction while the interface remains 'under glass' is the sensation of texture.

6.9
Vote Band App
This app concept from graduate Jacques Peacock allows users to instantly vote for their favourite acts during music events such as a 'Battle of the Bands.' To revolutionize the audience participation the app provides a social space where band details and special promotions can be aggregated through close connection to the Facebook platform. This augmented social space is still 'under the glass' of the touch screen but the user can feel instantaneously more informed about new music and respond through the touch of a finger on glass.

Touching interactions

For graphic designers working on print products the choice of physical materials, such as paper, card and cloth, are just as important a part of the visual communication as the typeface, kerning or colour. Up to this point, this has not been a factor for graphic designers engaged in web design, as the desktop consumption of a website firmly existed in the WIMP UI world. However, now that direct manipulation through touch is becoming dominant, the ways in which users interact with UIs is changing. Already, scientists are prototyping texture touch screens.

If this technology takes off, then it could have a huge impact on the graphic designer's role, and may be particularly challenging for those who have only designed for digital media. The non-digital design processes and skill sets learned at art college and on design degrees that focus on physical materials, such as packaging design, will be very useful for future UI design. Packaging design brings together the visual and the tactile senses into a graphic designed experience. Apple is a perfect example of creating an entire experience for their customer through their aesthetic packaging decisions. This aesthetic user experience, which seductively engages all the senses (especially the feel of the material) will need realizing on future touch-screen devices.

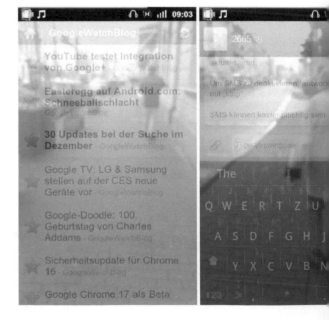

6.10
Transparent Screen
In this Transparent Screen Android app by Sascha Affolter, the touch screen can be made to appear transparent (by clever use of the camera), showing what's behind the user's phone through the Android apps that are currently running. This effect is not the same as AR, but it does allow the user to interact with the apps while walking – so that they can see what they're doing and where they're going at the same time. Although the app may have limited uses, it demonstrates the importance of an app working with the physicality of the display device.

6.10

This brings us back to the key role of visual communication in the UI design process. While scientists can technically approximate the sensation of texture, and developers will then translate that into code, the way that the sensation is communicated rests with the graphic designer. They can be instrumental in bringing to life the user experience of the UI through the visual and now (potentially) the feel of the UI, too.

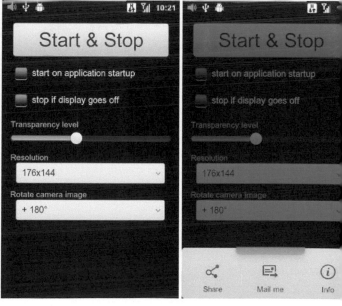

Role
**Managing Director,
Interface 3, UK**

Experience
**An award-winning
educational games
company with a
team of designers
and developers
who are
passionate about
producing playful,
novel, smart
multi-touch
games and toys.**

Web
interface3.com

**At Interface 3 you produce
smart multi-touch game
solutions for tablets and other
touch-screen technologies.
What is it about touch screens
that excites your designers?**

The beautiful thing about
touch is the sense that you
are directly manipulating
something. The idea that *there's*
something I *want* to *touch* is
more immediate and intuitive.
Children now expect things to
be touchable and swipeable!

**Do you see any other
technology that will affect
how we understand and
design interfaces in the
near future?**

If it's not touch screens then
it'll be Microsoft's Kinect (see
page 97). The Kinect has done
so much in terms of being
affordable (and now cross-
platform, thanks to the hackers).
I've seen smart TVs now where
they use a lot of gestures so
that you can select TV shows.
There is the idea of a connected
home, too. I've seen these
futuristic Microsoft videos where
every wall is a touch screen. I'm
not entirely sure we'll want that.
But I think with the portability of
tablet-based devices there'll be
so many more screens around
the home, and they'll be so
much more accessible.

'The beautiful thing
about touch is the sense
that you are directly
manipulating something.'
– Kate Ho

What is the issue with embedding so many touch screens in our homes and on our walls?

As with anything that you embed in the house, they get outdated so quickly. Whereas wall-mount an iPad and… perfect. Two years later you need a new iPad? Take it out and plug a new one in. I think they'll be slightly limited, but not because we don't want them around us, but more that we want to keep them up to date.

So the portability of a touch-screen device is important?

The portability is just amazing. I think there'll always be a place, especially in the workplace, for laptops for when you want to do *work*. But I think when you need computers-on-the-go (and let's admit it, we all need computers-on-the-go in general because we're so used to having Google Maps and real-time information) that those devices will become even more portable over time.

Is it helpful to see laptops as being predominantly used for production of 'content', while touch-screen tablets are more for consumption of 'content'?

With production-based stuff, you want that picture *'right there'* or that text *'right there'*. Whereas when you're consuming, you very rarely do very detailed actions.

That hooks into the idea of the context stuff, because then you have to be more intelligent as you can't place 70 buttons (as in an old TV remote control) on a screen. On a touch screen, realistically, you can only put 12 buttons on a screen because each button has to fit the size of a finger. We're starting to use that way of thinking, so now it becomes second nature to us when we design.

Do you think that the sense of texture will be added to future touch-screen technologies?

It would be strange if we never moved that bit further and added a sense of texture, and why shouldn't it happen? The tech is now getting to a stage where I think the scientists have worked out how it can be done. It's whether it can be done at an affordable price and can be scaled. Why wouldn't you texture your interface so that it's inviting to touch? And with iPads, it's really messing with peoples' heads regarding the visual affordances, because how do you represent the visual affordance of texture as a result? This is our first stab at it, and I think over the next couple of years you'll see improvements on the design as newer, braver types of designers start to challenge the possibilities even more.

Project
**The Macallan
Microsoft Surface
at Schiphol
Airport**

Design team
**Whitespace,
Edinburgh, UK
www.
whitespacers.com**

Implementation
team
**Interface3,
Edinburgh, UK
www.interface3.
com**

Client
Edrington

The project

The Macallan Scotch whisky distillery was founded in 1824, in the heart of Speyside, and today promotes itself as a luxury premium spirit. Whitespace was commissioned by Edrington to use cutting-edge technologies to build a UI to help consumers to engage with one of the world's leading malts at point of purchase.

Whitespace's objective was to communicate the brand's reputation through the use of interactivity, video and compelling visual communication in an interface within an international travel retail environment. The Macallan's 'The 1824 Collection' is exclusive to Travel Retail and therefore only available at certain locations, such as Amsterdam's Schiphol Airport whisky shop. In collaboration with Interface3, the Microsoft PixelSense (Surface 2) touch-screen platform was chosen.

**6.11
Initial scamp –
product-specific tasting notes**
In an early visual, the design team communicated the user experience to the client.

**6.12
User journey – from surface
to data capture**
The team created a wireframe demonstrating how the interactive flow through the interaction would take the user to their desired content.

The touch-screen interaction

The Microsoft PixelSense touch-screen surface uses Windows 7 multi-touch and .Net technologies, which allowed the design team to exploit the object-recognition capability of the technology. The team, comprising principally of Iain Valentine (Creative Director), Charlie Bell (Graphic Design Director) and Johnny Lewery (Motion Designer), designed the interface so the customer could take a touch-screen journey through the story behind The Macallan. Multiple customers could operate the UI selecting bottles from The 1824 Collection, placing them on the touch-screen surface to interactively reveal each bottle's contextual information. Customers could then experience how the whisky is made, browse whisky tasting notes and videos at their own pace.

6.11

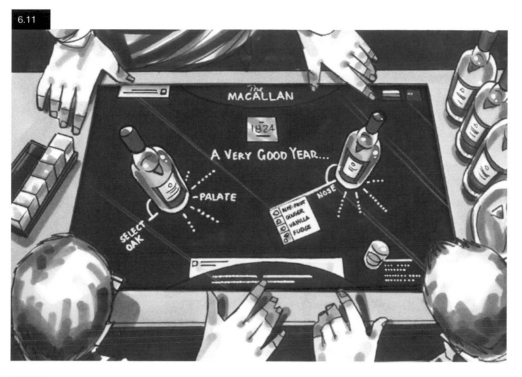

6.12

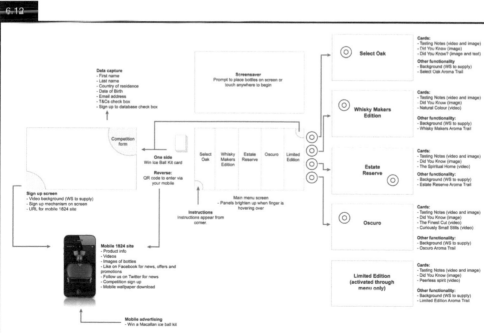

The designed user experience

The design team had quite a few things they needed to understand before designing the UI: the Macallan brand, their target audience, the technology's opportunities and constraints, the location for, and the implementation and testing of the UI. They engaged in site visits to both the distillery and Schiphol Airport's whisky shop, immersing themselves in the whisky production process – including tasting a few drams (glasses of whisky).

By engaging with the developers from Interface3, the design team ensured that their workshopping and brainstorming of ideas would not only exploit the full potential of the PixelSense touch-screen technology, but their final concept would also be technically achievable. For example, the technology relied on light sensitivity for object recognition to work, so the final interface's surface would need to be precisely calibrated to the context of Schiphol Airport's whisky shop. This led the team to visit Schiphol Airport. This in-depth testing of the UI, from the initial prototyping of ideas through to the user testing of the final design, gave the team valuable insight into verifying their design decisions for the visual communication of the interactive user experience.

The graphic designer in the project

A visual communication perspective was present throughout the entire UI project. The main design team was made up of experienced UI graphic designers having designed interfaces and apps for clients such as UK television broadcaster Channel 4. Collaborating with Whitespace's in-house development team and Interface3, the graphic designers contributed greatly to a successful user experience using cutting-edge touch-screen technology.

From conception through to the coding and the testing of the UI, the graphic designers ensured that the visual communication of interaction was a success for the entire interface project. The research from the distillery and airport visits revealed important insights that would otherwise have been missed; these insights added a richness of detail to the interactive design. In doing so, Whitespace delivered a user experience that smoothly and effectively implemented a branded touch-screen experience, which reflected the luxury positioning of The Macallan and answered the brief provided.

6.13

6.14

6.13
Interactive for Oscuro bottle
The discussions with Interface3 flagged that users still needed to be able to browse the surface without having to place the bottle on the screen.

6.14
Select oak cask
'Aroma trails' (images of flavours) from the whisky appear to flow from the tip of the finger touching the screen.

Premise

In this final exercise, the focus is on consolidating your visual communication skills in the concept design of an augmented reality (AR) app. The exercise will engage many skills needed to design interfaces: research, user-research, information architecture, visual hierarchy, navigation, content, graphic design for digital media, designing an aesthetic experience, modularizing and localization.

The aim of this exercise is to create a concept design for an AR app on a touch-screen smartphone showing a walk-through of the information overlays within a panoramic view of a scene.

Outcomes

This final exercise helps you to understand how functionality and usability are both important for visual communication. By working within the constraints of a small screen with information that would be dynamically accessed in real time, there is a need for a 'Goldilocks' solution that is functional and that visually communicates the required information in such a way that will be usable by another human being. The exercise should help consolidate all your visual communication skills with technical constraints to help you to design successful interfaces, which create positive aesthetic user experiences.

Exercise

This exercise is broken down into four parts.

Part 1: Discovery

Before beginning this exercise you will need to:

— Make a panorama photograph of a scene in your locale.

— Research some contextual information about the locale to add as AR overlays. From the research, decide the purpose of your AR app concept by choosing a specific information theme (for example, the nearest transport stops).

— Decide who your target audience is and create a set of user personas to help you understand what they will need from the app. This may make you revise your concept.

Part 2: Adding the panorama into the smartphone template

— Once you have your panoramic scene, place it into your smartphone template (see image 6.15 overleaf).

— In the template, the smartphone needs to sit in the top layer with another layer below to contain the concept design's AR walk-throughs.

— You will have to expand the width of the canvas to match the width of the panorama, and may also have to reduce the size of your smartphone if it is too big. Don't enlarge either image – you'll lose quality.

Part 3: Overlaying information

— Depending on the concept you've chosen and the quality of research you've done to find out information about the environment, you will now design a UI as an AR overlay.

— Try out several concepts before deciding on one UI design.

— Choose the strongest concept and place it into your smartphone template over your panorama scene (see image 6.16).

— Overlay ALL the AR information you have to the file in a new layer (see image 6.17).

Part 4: Finalizing the design concept

— Through a period of design iterations, revise your design, and where necessary, change the amount of information displayed (see image 6.18). Good copywriting may help here.

— Try printing the file out and make a paper prototype to test with some target users.

— Once you're satisfied that the concept is working, finalize it into a design concept that you could show a client.

6.15

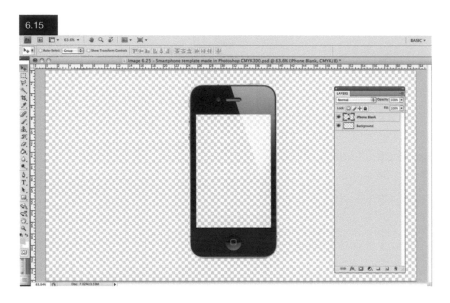

6.16

6.15
Smartphone template
The smartphone needs to sit on
a top layer in Adobe Photoshop
(or similar software) with another
layer below to contain the
concept design's AR
walk-throughs.

6.16
Adding the panorama
Once you have your panoramic
scene, place it into your
smartphone template. Don't
enlarge either image – you'll
lose quality.

6.17

6.18

6.17
Overlaying information
Overlay ALL the information you
have to the file in a new layer.

6.18
Finalizing the design concept
Through a period of design
iterations, revise your design,
and where necessary, change
the amount of information
displayed (good copywriting
may help here).

Abjads
A writing system, such as Arabic or Hebrew, where each symbol refers to a consonant, leaving the reader to add the vowels.

Action safe area
Approximately 95% of a TV screen is what is deemed 'action safe', as TV screens tend to cut off the edges of the picture through overscanning.

Adjustment layers
A layer that contains an effect, such as brightness or saturation, that is applied to all the layers that sit below it.

Aesthetics
This means more than just a particular style or type of UI design. Aesthetics is integral to the human experience as it is a perception and judgement on the quality of beauty. It is heavily invested in the experiences one encounters in the world. What is judged as aesthetic is fluid. Current cultural norms and societal values may change ('the new black' or 'what's cool' trends).

Affordance
see *Visual affordance*

Algorithm
In programming, this is a computational procedure that is based on mathematical logic that if correctly applied solves a problem.

Alpha channel
Controls the opacity of a colour or image. 100%: fully visible, 0%: invisible.

Analogous colours
These colours sit next to each other on the colour wheel, and work well with each other as they share a similar part of the colour spectrum (for example, green, blue, purple).

Android
Google's mobile operating system for smartphones and PC tablets.

Anti-aliasing
A blurring of two coloured pixels with a third pixel that is a mix of the two to create the illusion of smoothness, compensating for the stepped nature of pixels.

App(s)
Short for Application(s), usually referring to software to be used on a smartphone or tablet.

AR
see *Augmented reality (AR)*

Ascenders
The vertical stem of a lower-case letter like 'h' that extends above the x-height of a typeface.

Assets
The elements that make up a design, which will be placed into the structure of the UI.

Augmented reality (AR)
A technology that blurs the digital world with the real world by digitally overlaying a level of additional information onto what can be seen. This is currently done using a digital device, such as a smartphone. It enhances the experience of a real-world environment in real time.

Back-end ordering system
A database system in eCommerce websites that processes orders, payment transactions, and transportation.

Bandwidth
Think broadband, 3G and Wi-Fi as this refers to the channel through which data is delivered via telecommunication. It is measured through bits per second and a 'bit' is a single piece of information.

BD
Abbreviation for Blu-ray Disc, an optical disc format that is replacing DVDs.

Bitmaps
An image created through colouring each pixel using file formats, such as JPG, PNG and GIF.

Bleed
Any part of the design that extends off the screen edges.

Body copy
Written content that isn't a header, caption or link that forms the main information parts of a UI page.

Brainstorm
An active dialogue within a team to discover design problems and then mindmap design solutions.

Calls to action
These are visual communications that inform the user that they need to choose or do something within the interaction, such as a submit button.

Cascading Style Sheets (CSS)
Used in conjunction with HTML and PHP they control the structure of a website. This code defines the styling of a website's layout.

CMYK
Colour space using cyan, magenta, yellow and black used in print.

Co-design
A design methodology that is community-centred where designers work directly with representatives of the people who will be served by a designed outcome. The 'co' in co-design can mean cooperative, community or collaborative.

Code
In the context of this book, code has been used as a catch-all term to describe all the programming languages used in UI design, from simple markup HTML to more advanced C++ and everything in between.

Coder
A programmer (see also Developer).

Comp
This is a working version of the final design. In this book it refers to the digital file (Photoshop, Illustrator, Fireworks, InDesign etc) that has the UI structure and assets composited into an underlying grid on separate layers, grouped and labelled accordingly.

Complementary colours
These colours sit opposite each other on the colour wheel (like red/green). Choosing complementary colours helps calm our visual system.

Contextual navigation
Navigation that may only be available in a particular area of the UI, on a particular subject page or may only become unlocked within a process. An example is the options on each window of a software installation where the buttons change their action calls depending on what step of the process has been reached.

Contrasting colours
Colours that are from different parts of the colour wheel (such as a red and blue) and can be effective in drawing attention.

CSS
see *Cascading Style Sheets*

CSS3
The latest version of CSS that adds a whole level of styling control for a designer.

Deconstruction
An act of analysing and breaking down an existing design to understand how it is constructed. This allows you to see and understand the design decisions that have been taken and how the design has been structured.

Demographic
A marketing term that describes the common characteristics of a group of people sorted by age, sex, class, etc.

Descenders
The vertical stem of a lower-case letter like 'g' that extends below the baseline of a typeface.

Developer
A programmer who produces the code for the UI design. They may be front-end developers concerned with coding markup and styling for web or mobile UIs (HTML, XHTML, HTML 5, Javascript, XML, CSS). They may also be back-end developers concerned with programming the game engines, content management systems, data delivery (Python, Ruby, C, PhP, Cocoa, VisualBAsic, AJAX, jQuery, MySQL).

Dithered
Digital mixing of colours pixel by pixel to aid display,

Em
An em is equal to the width of a capital M and relative to the size of a typeface's current font size. It has finer size increments and scales well.

Eye tracking
User-testing that uses camera technology to capture eye movements around an interface on a screen generating data on what was looked at to test the effectiveness of a UI's visual hierarchy. It is not just the eye movement that is measured, but also the duration of time spent looking at each element on the screen,

Fluid grids
The fluid control of gridded content that can resize the widths and heights of each element relative to each other for different devices.

Flush left
Straight alignment of body copy to the left-hand margin allowing the right-hand side to be 'ragged.'

Fonts
Often confused with a typeface - a typeface is a family of fonts. The font is a classification of a style of typeface such as roman, condensed, italic or bold.See also *Typeface.*

Functionality
How a UI works focusing on the combination of the technology used, the look and feel of the UI on a device, and the underlying code that makes the device work.

Global navigation
Navigation that is available from every page of the UI. Examples of this form of navigation would include links to the home page, to help, to print etc.

Graphical user interface (GUI)
A user interface that uses bitmapped graphics. Through the graphic design and use of visual metaphors, it visually communicates the interface's navigation, the interaction and content.

Grid
The grid is an underlying framework that graphic design has used effectively to structure visual communication. A grid helps to place content and navigation in a controlled way to aid visual communication.

Gridded structure
A gridded structure aids the comprehension of the user in distinguishing the visual hierarchy of navigation and content.

GUI
see *Graphical User Interface*

Gutters
The gaps between columns in a grid.

Hexadecimal values
Colour on web-based UIs is controlled by the code through a conversion of the RGB values into a hexadecimal value. The values that make up the range of hexadecimal colours begin at zero and go up to nine, and use the letters A to F.

Hierarchical gridded structure
A design's visual hierarchy laid out in a grid in a digital comp file.

Hot spots
In eye-tracking, the areas on a screen where eye movements are recorded lingering the most.

HTML
Hyper-text Markup Language. Code that defines the structure of a web-based interface.

HTML5
A new development of HTML that eliminates the need to install third party plug-ins in browsers and allows the code to control more interactive multimedia assets that were formerly controlled by Adobe Flash.

Hypertext
The fundamental basic foundation of interactive design. It is the linking of text within a document or across different documents. This text is displayed as underlined, and usually blue in its un-clicked state, turning to purple after it has been visited.

IA
see *Information architecture*

Icon
Interface tools that visually focus attention and communicate in a concise and simple way a call to action in the interface by using an understandable visual metaphor.

Iconography
The visual grammar of the symbols used in the design of icons for a UI.

Ideation
The initial idea-generating phase of the design process where lots of ideas for the project outcome are proposed through brainstorming.

Information architecture (IA)
A process of research, analysis and evaluation to communicate to the UI design team the UI's interactive structure, revealing an optimum navigation pathway through the content to ensure user and client goals are met. The IA provides information as to what-content-goes-where and what-needs-to-link-to-what.

Interactive kiosk
A static interactive screen found in situ within public arenas for public use.

Interface
see *User interface*

Invisible interface
When an aesthetic user experience has been achieved, the user's awareness of the interface itself will disappear from their conscious attention.

iOS
Apple's mobile operating system for iPhone and iPad.

Iterative design
A design process that understands that great design doesn't just appear, it emerges from a creative experimental process. This is cyclical and follows repetition of an ideation and designing phase, followed by prototyping and testing the design. This reveals areas for improvement and modification in the design, which begins another phase of designing and user testing until a successful design outcome has been achieved within the deadline and budget set by the client.

Iterative process
see *Iterative design*

Internationalization
'The design and development of a product, application or document content that enables easy localization for target audiences that vary in culture, region or language.'
– *World Wide Web Consortium*

JavaScript
A scripting language used to create interactivity within a web-based UI, such as validating forms, image rollovers and to open pop-up windows.

jQuery
A JavaScript library of functions and methods that helps to simplify the interaction, event handling and animations within an HTML document.

Kerning
The spacing of letters within a word that allows the adjustment of one letter nearer or farther away from its closest neighbour.

Leading
An increase or decrease in the vertical spaces between baselines, which can have dramatic affects on legibility.

Linear
Navigation within a UI that follows a sequential order, such as page 1 then page 2, 3, 4.

Localization
'The adaptation of a product, application or document content to meet the language, cultural and other requirements of a specific target market (a 'locale').'
– World Wide Web Consortium

Logographic
A writing system (such as Chinese) that can be read vertically or horizontally.

Markup
Syntax used, as in coding language, such as HTML (and variants XML and XHTML), for defining elements in web pages or data files. Markup uses tags in the code before and after each element to define the element such as <title></title>.

Media query
see jQuery

Metaphor
The transfer of meaning from one object to designate another object with that meaning (this different thing represents this actual thing).

Modularity
The process of designing using asset sizes that can be coded once and reused as many times as required in the UI.

Modules
UI elements that are repeatable components with ratio defined sizes on both their x-axis and y-axis, which are then reusable.

MySQL
A relational database management system used in conjunction with PHP to dynamically add, remove and modify data in a database connected to a UI.

Navigation contextual structure
A way of grouping and visualizing content in the IA through content associations rather than a hierarchical gridded structure, which shows each navigation level in neat rows.

Navigation pathway
The route through an interface to access the content where features of higher primary importance will be presented to the user first, with secondary features held in reserve.

Negative space
The spaces between assets and information in a UI, which allows the hierarchy of the design to be revealed and the user to quickly find the content they want.

Non-linear
Navigation that does not follow a sequential order, but can jump to any content or page within the navigational structure of the UI or outside it if it uses hypertextual links.

Participatory design
Built on the four principles of cooperating, experimenting, contextualizing and iterating. It is an approach that emphasizes active user participation in computer system development.

Personas
see User personas

PHP (Hypertext Preprocessor)
A scripting language that defines the structure of a website that is read from a server and displayed as HTML code in a browser. This makes PHP secure enough to access secure information and databases (in conjunction with MySQL).

Pixel
A single square that can be one of over 65,000 colours on a screen display.

Platform
Usually refers to the operating system, such as iOS, OSX, Windows and Android that controls the device that a UI is displayed on.

Progress bars
When some UIs load on certain devices, the rate of loading is displayed as a linear graphical line that changes colour in relation to the percentage of the UI that has been loaded.

Prototype
A mock-up of a proposed system or concept for inspection, testing and guidance.

QR codes
see Quick response codes

Qualitative data
Information that is more concerned with understanding the qualities of something. This form of data is collected using a variety of social science methodologies including ethnography, phenomenology, anthropology, grounded theory, hermeneutics, content analysis, critical theory and discourse analysis.

Quantitative data
Information that is verifiable in the form of statistical analysis of figures, measurements and quantities.

Quick response codes
A barcode with the capacity of holding tens of thousands of bits of information and acting as a shortcut to web-based content from the physical world. It is printed as a square code that can be found on posters, leaflets, labels, books, magazines or any conceivable object. The QR code is scanned with an app on a smartphone, which takes the user to the related web-based data.

Responsive design
A web design methodology using CSS3 jQueries to determine the screen size and capability of the target device that the website will be displayed on, and then the code resizes the UI design to suit the detected device.

Return on investment (ROI)
The client who commissions a UI will invest money into the interface and will want to see a result from that investment. This may mean an increased financial return or more people using the interface. The client should state their requirements early in the initial conversations, and the UX designer and information architect will have responsibility in how the ROI will be measured.

RGB
Colour space using red, green and blue in digital display.

RGBA
In CSS3, the RGB colour value with an added alpha channel value referenced by the A.

ROI
see Return on investment

Screen resolution
The screen quality determined by how many pixels per inch (ppi) will be displayed. The higher the density, the better the screen quality.

Semiotics
An underlying theory on which successful visual communication is built. There is a connection between what you see (signifier) and what it means (signified). These two parts – the visual signifier and its signified meaning – form a semiotic sign.

Server-side programming (or scripting)
The online fulfilment of a user request executed by a script on a web server and displayed in the user's browser.

Skinning
The reduction of graphic design for digital media from rich visual communication throughout the design process to 'visual design'. The skinning of code refers to the graphic designer only being brought in at the end of the design process after the code has been written.

Smart objects
Within Photoshop, these are layers that preserve an image's source content which can be edited as a layer without affecting the original bitmap or vector image.

Tabs
A navigational device based on an office filing system metaphor to indicate navigation options. This helps the user to understand where they are within the interactive structure, and know where they can next proceed.

Text safe area
Approximately 90% of a TV screen is deemed 'text safe' where text is always viewable despite TV screens losing information off the edges of the picture through overscanning.

Third-party plug-ins
Additional software added to existing applications to augment that application's range of options. The most obvious plug-in is Flash Player, which is added to a browser to view Flash content.

Tracking
The horizontal increasing or decreasing of the spaces between each letter in a word; it can have different effects on readability and comprehension.

Trackpad
The input area on a laptop.

Triadic relationship
A three-colour scheme that is equally spaced using an equilateral triangle.

Typeface
A typeface is a style of letters including upper case, lower case, numbers and glyphs. Examples of typefaces include Times, Helvetica, Verdana and Courier.

Typography
Aids the communication of text through the deliberate and thoughtful selection of the most suitable typeface (at the correct size for the reader) by manipulating word height, letter style and spacing between words, letters and lines.

Uploader
A small app or widget that transfers digital files from one computer device or peripheral to another computer.

Usability testing
Testing evaluates the accessibility and usability of an interface. Testing the UI at different design stages reveals any usability problems that need addressing. Ideally, three or four people (not design staff) should test the UI design. Each user will perform the same task and this generates questions that demand solutions.

Usability testing facility
Usability testing doesn't need expensive facilities. It can be conducted with minimum equipment and a video camera. Watching the user remotely from another room via a video link allows the design team to observe how the UI is working. Viewing via a camera that the user is not aware of, nor distracted by, allows for more natural behaviour to be observed.

User advocate
In UI design, the UX designer ensures that the user is championed in the design process.

User experience (UX)
A successful interaction for the user.

User-facing names
Text written in words the user would understand instead of using technical terms.

User interface (UI)
An interface is a point of contact between two entities. In a user interface, this is effectively the visual interaction between a human and a computer.

User personas
An important tool in the designer's toolkit. It is an archetype (not a stereotype) created to represent the target user(s) in a form that will inspire the design team. It takes the form of a profile with a name, an image and various amounts of information on each type of user. The use of personas at the ideation stage helps the design team identify their target audience, summarizing user motivations, expectations, experience, knowledge and desires.

UX
see *User experience*

Vectors
One form of digital image that does not lose image integrity in resizing. They are mathematically defined, and infinitely scalable without loss of quality.

Virtual reality (VR)
A term describing an environment that a person can become immersed in, explore and interact with, which is wholly computer generated.

Visual affordance
The communication of interactivity in a UI indicating calls to action that lead to a successful outcome.

Visual hierarchy
The headers, navigation and content are layered from high importance, to secondary and then tertiary importance, affording an effortless flow through the interface by communicating what is accessible, what is interactive, and what to do next.

Visual rhythm
The balancing of the hierarchy to help the user's effortless flow through the interface.

VR
see *Virtual reality*

White space
see *Negative space*

Widgets
Mini-applications used to perform specific tasks that can be embedded within a larger UI (for example, a voting box on a website).

WIMPs
Traditionally GUIs have been designed for interaction via windows, icons, menus and a pointer.

Wireframing
A proposed layout using nothing more than lines, boxes and basic text to show possible frameworks for the visual hierarchy, navigation priorities and suitable content areas. It is a method that takes the IA and considers the technical platforms that the UI will be accessed from. They are not the final design that just needs 'colouring in'.

x-axis
The horizontal width of the screen.

x-height
The vertical height of a lower case letter like 'x' not counting letters with ascenders (like 'h') or descenders (like 'y').

y-axis
The vertical height of the screen.

Page numbers in *italics* denote
illustrations.

I'd like to dedicate this book to the late James Russell – friend, mentor and uncle.

Without the help and support of the following people I wouldn't have been able to write this book:

Paula O'Connell for the initial advice and support that helped me write a very strong proposal. Fellow lecturer Alan MacFarlane and his 50gb online storage for saving my three PowerPoint lectures on the very subject of this book that I foolishly deleted from my own hard drive. My proofreading friends: Tony Hardwick, Kristin Kramer and Mel Owen.

I would also like to thank the staff at Fairchild Books for giving me this opportunity to write a book on the very subject I have been researching for a decade. Thanks to Georgia Kennedy for sourcing me with the commission, and my editor Jacqui Sayers for her patience and extremely helpful guidance through the publishing process.